INFORMAL LEARNING IN ELEMENTARY SCHOOLS

Danny G. Fulks

University Press
of America™

LB
1029
.06
F845
1978

INFORMAL LEARNING IN ELEMENTARY SCHOOLS

CONTENTS   PAGE

CONTRIBUTORS

Becky Burris
Jo Ann Gainer
Beverly Ours

-

ACKNOWLEDGEMENTS

The Cabell County Public Schools
Huntington, West Virginia

The College of Education
Marshall University
Huntington, West Virginia

The several students who not only made some of these ideas work
but contributed many ideas of their own.

Joyce Wright
Sondra Jarrell
Kathy Dickerson
Bridget Morgan, Editor and special assistant
Harold E. Lewis, Jr.

If one could drive the great philosophers and
theorists into a corner and hold a .38 to their
head, they would have to admit that few things
were certain, consistently moral, or predictable.

DF

Sandy, Candy, Cathy

I concluded, finally, partly in self-defense, that
learning could take place without the child having
to communicate constantly with the teacher.

From Homework: Required Reading for Teachers and Parents by
Gloria Channon. Copyright (c) 1970 by Outerbridge & Dienstfrey.
Published by E. P. Dutton and reprinted with their permission.

As an addendum to the prologue of this book, the author believes that the following article by Fred M. Hechinger contains vital information for the advocators of informal learning specifically and for educators in general. It is presented here in its entirety.

REAPPRAISING THE OPEN CLASSROOM

An English report that is likely to dominate educational debate in the United States as much as it will in Britain in the years ahead has dampened the current highly publicized enthusiasm for "open" (also known as "informal" or "progressive") classrooms. In summary, the study shows the following:

-- Formal teaching methods tend to achieve superior results, not only in basic skills but even in creative areas.

-- Formal teaching is more successful with children who have a high level of anxiety or neurosis, while informal classrooms seem to aggravate their problems.

-- Formal teaching achieves academic goals without harm to children's emotional and social development.

These findings add up to a pedagogic bombshell. The rival advocates of traditional education and progressive education have long been feuding bitterly, each claiming that the other is the cause of most educational and social disasters. The traditionalists blame everything from illiteracy to moral decline on the progressives; the latter hold the traditionalists responsible not only for children's reluctance to learn but also for all manner of trauma and psychological damage, and even accuse them of fostering a drift toward authoritarian politics.

Over the years, the pendulum has swung back and forth, in classrooms and in public debate. After the heyday of progressivism, in the 1930s, conservative counterattacks reached their maximum force in 1957, in Sputnik's red glare, amid charges that progressive education in America had allowed the Soviets to achieve their lead in space. (Actually, many of the Russian scientists engaged in space research in the 1940s and 1950s learned their basic skills in the 1920s and early 1930s--the Soviet Union's progressive-education era.)

At any rate, academic rigor and the three R's came back with a vengeance in the conservative Fifties, only to be challenged again, in the radical Sixties, as being oppressive, joyless, and autocratic. But while American educational progressivism had in

1

the past been based largely on the homegrown models of such pioneers as Horace Mann and John Dewey, the latest version was imported from England. Britain's open classrooms became the foundation for the American reform movement of the 1960s. American educators returned from their pilgrimages to British schools with glowing reports about teaching that "really worked."

Now the British themselves have raised serious and responsible questions about that assumption. What gives special significance to the report--Teaching Styles and Pupil Progress, by Neville Bennett (Open Books, London)--is that the entire research crew responsible for the study set out ideologically on the side of progressive theory. The team, associated with the University of Lancaster, took as its sample the third and fourth grades of 871 primary schools in the counties of Lancashire and Cumbria. The region includes industrial cities and rural areas, state schools and church schools, old schools and new.

What should be made of the report? Conservative educators, who are riding high on the resultant wave of civic and political reaction, are undoubtedly ready to use the findings as a justification for banishing all vestiges of progressive education. The consequence would be another extreme swing of the pendulum toward the kind of reactionary pedagogy that has in the past, because of its own grim deficiencies, inevitably prepared the way for eqaully uncompromising progressive countermeasures.

But what the Lancaster report shows--and this is most readily overlooked in simplistic and partisan discussions--is that there is more to this educational controversy than an "either/or" choice between opposites. Instead of identifying just two diametrically different teaching styles, the observers noted a variety of at least 12 distinct styles, and a mix of many more.

It was precisely when the open classroom functioned in its extreme form, without any firm structure to shape the children's learning, that the results were most unsatisfactory. Stating it another way: While some educationists view formal grammar and creativity as being incompatible, the study found the very opposite to be true--formal teachers and those who mixed formal and informal styles achieved success in both grammar and creativity.

Common sense suggests that there are grave psychological disadvantages in the polar extremes of drill-master traditionalism and super-permissive progressivism. And this is confirmed by the study's finding that the most successful teachers use a "mix" of formal and informal styles--a comforting thought for those who want schools to be pleasant places and educationally effective at the same time.

2

This hopeful view of education is borne out by one statistically odd but significant observation: one lone progressive teacher in the entire large sample went sharply counter to the trends by producing uniformly superior results. Her case deserves special attention:

A woman in her middle thirties, with ten years' experience, she saw to it that the amount of time spent on English and mathematics within her informal classroom was at least equal to that devoted to these "basics" in formal classrooms. Informality to her did not mean that the teacher had a lesser obligation to determine standards and priorities. Free to select and produce her own materials, she constantly but subtly combined creative topics with the study of grammar. Asked what motivated the children to succeed, she bluntly said that she herself was the main incentive: "They know I'll be pleased if they do well."

When told of the children's high scores on a standardized test, the teacher expressed no surprise. "I would be disappointed," she said, "if a class went out without feeling that all the children achieved something. . . . At the beginning of the year they groaned when they were to do math, but by the end of the year they liked it."

In her classroom, progressive ideology was never allowed to get in the way of the work ethic. "Whilst there [is] a lot of emphasis on the social aspects in school, the children are encouraged to be work-minded right from the infants." And her view was confirmed by the report's general conclusion that "a clear link appears to emerge between work activity. . . and progress." In fact, lack of work activity in some of the informal classrooms was found to retard the progress of both slow and bright children. Merely talking about the work or socializing as a substitute for work simply does not provide enough incentive for the independent effort and "discovery" learning hoped for by advocates of informal education. As Jerome Bruner, one of America's leading experts on the psychology of learning, cautioned in 1961: "Discovery, like surprise, favors a well-prepared mind."

The Lancaster report confirms what many non-ideological, middle-of-the-road education experts have long believed--that it is far more difficult to teach effectively under informal conditions than it is in a structured classroom. Informal teaching requires a suitable personality and extraordinary skill--a teacher who is "dedicated, highly organized, able to work flexibly, able to plan ahead, and willing to spend a great deal of extra time in preparatory work."

Such requirements add up to a formidable hurdle in any effort to apply progressive ideals to mass education. In an enterprise that calls for armies of teachers, it may never be

possible to provide enough recruits with the dedication, sophis-
tication, sublety, and skill needed to turn ideal into reality.
Without the teacher's capacity (despite the _appearance_ of child-
dominated informality) to remain in control of the priorities and
activities not only of the class but of each child, the open
classroom becomes an educational quagmire. Children in need of
firm support will flounder; they may momentarily have fun, but
eventually their frustration over inadequate skills will get in
the way of their learning. This is precisely why the study found
that informality aggravates neurotic behavior and why, in the
words of one expert, "it is predictable that children with a low
toleration for ambiguity and uncertainty would find an open classroom that operates successfully for [other] children extremely
threatening and anxiety-provoking."

These caveats are hardly new, though they have recently been
forgotten. The fact is that in the 1920s, when Dewey's progressive classroom stressed "group-mindedness," or socialization,
often at the expense of academic emphasis, parents from the
ethnic ghettos raised their voices in protest. Their children,
they said, in contrast to the sheltered offspring of the rich,
had plenty of group activity in the streets; what they needed was
the capacity to deal with letters and numbers.

In spite of the _Lancaster study's_ essentially moderate conclusions, one of the troubling prospects is this: Because its
findings are certain to be widely quoted, they will be even more
widely abused. They _may, unfortunately, come to serve as a rally-_
ing cry for leading education back to the stultifying and authori-
tarian teaching styles that are currently--and mistakenly--
considered by so many to be the royal road to learning the three
_R's_.

This is emphatically _not_ what the report recommends. "_It is_
surely time," its authors caution, "_to ignore the rhetoric which_
would have us believe that informal methods are pernicious and
permissive, and that the most accurate description of formal
methods is that found in Dickens's _Hard Times_."

But beyond that reasonable call for moderation, the report
raises some hard questions: What aspects of formal teaching are
responsible for success in the basic skills, and how can they be
incorporated in a more informal and congenial setting? How can
teaching be reformed to provide enough structure for the anxious
and enough stimulation for the bright? How can conservatives be
made to understand that making school enjoyable does not subvert
learning--and progressives to admit that enthusiasm over their
ideas is not enough to make them work?

One point emerges from the study with the utmost clarity:
to identify progressive education as the root of all academic

failure is sheer nonsense, if for no other reason than the fact
that only a small minority of teachers have ever adopted an
exclusively informal approach. In the area covered by the study,
for example, no more than 17 percent of the teachers could be
classified as progressives; 25 percent taught formally; while the
majority used mixed styles, incorporating formal and informal
practices. A careful poll in the United States would very likely
yield similar results.

During my efforts as a young reporter in the early 1950s to
find some answers to the controversy between progressives and
traditionalists (which then raged in the political arena as well
as in the pedagogical), I followed the progress of two first-
grade classrooms in the same Queens, New York, public school.
Both teachers, though at opposite ends of the progressive-
traditional spectrum, were superb practitioners. Each was
clearly loved and respected by the children. At year's end, it
was impossible to distinguish between the two groups' achieve-
ments. The outcome reflected neither praise nor condemnation for
either of the two ideologies; it was simply a celebration of good,
professional teaching.

So, in the end, is the Lancaster report. But since the
unmistakable implication of its findings is the infinetly greater
difficulty of achieving good informal education within the grave
limitations of mass education, progressive educationists must now
recognize "that the burden is increasingly upon them to accommodate their enthusiasm to [the report's] data." What the bombshell
shattered is not an ideal, but the false promise of a panacea.

From Saturday Review, March 19, 1977. Used by permission.

I am coming to believe that if you set out to
teach you'll never learn; and I know from my
own experience that when I set out to learn I
always end up teaching.

Willie Claflin

Prologue

This book represents the West Virginia version of a movement
in elementary and middle schools which is congruent with what has
come to be called open education or informal learning in the
United States. The history and theories of informal learning are
briefly reviewed in the first chapter. It appears to the author
that an overview of the psychological and physical aspects of informal learning was needed to establish a rationale. The central
theme of this book, however, is to simplify the theories and to
get into the practical kinds of teaching strategies which will be
effective in any geographic and ethnic locale.

The information and suggestions presented here are neither
revolutionary nor idealistic. They are practical, convenient, and
for the most part, non-controversial. The author has attempted to
respond to the complaints of practicing teachers that educational
jargon and theoretical precepts are acceptable in schools of education but are often impractical in the real world of students,
school administrators, and parents. The practices suggested in
this book are based on ideas about how one can best foster a cli-
mate of maximum learning and psychological security within the
public schools.

The goals of informal learning are acceptable goals in communities everywhere. Activity classrooms can be implemented in
West Virginia, East Tennessee, Chicago, and Los Angeles. The only
significant differences in program implementation are to be found
in the flavor of the local culture which is as it should be. The
author believes, in fact, that local themes should formulate the
curriculum base for early education no matter what locale is involved. The public schools belong to the people and we are probably deceived when we believe that the professionals have the
answers or that new educational practices can be implemented
behind the public's back.

Practicing teachers and their students have been greatly
involved in putting this book together. As the author and the
teachers worked together in the schools on informal learning
techniques, they found that the incorporation of learning centers
into once traditional classrooms was a practical step toward the
goal of developing classrooms which were more open.

<u>Informal Learning in Elementary Schools</u> is designed to provide practical suggestions and ideas for students majoring in early childhood education, special education, elementary education, and middle school programs relative to the development and implementation of informal classrooms through the use of learning centers. This book is also designed to serve as a learning center text for practicing elementary teachers.

In order to move toward an informal approach to learning, teachers must confront the problems involved in making the transition from formalized instruction. Learning center development—a pragmatic approach to change—in one way teachers can implement methods which reflect the latest knowledge about how children learn.

Cynics will be comforted by the fact that to date learning centers have not revolutionized education. One should remember, however, that neither did the Joplin plan, nongraded schools, individualized instruction, programmed instruction, learning packages, remedial reading, special education, Title IV, personalized education, prescribed programs, developmental skills, modular scheduling, team teaching, competency based programs, or a hundred other professionalized systems. Informal learning, whatever it is, seems to be somewhat congruent with the current goals of public education. Learning centers in elementary classrooms are, therefore, worth knowing about because in some remote areas of the Western world they exist; and under certain conditions, which are hard to define, they work. Winston Churchill once said that history would be kind to his generation because that was the way he intended to write it. The same idea could be related to learning centers. They are significant if only because there seems to be good argument for them.

The reader will notice that several friends and colleagues have made contributions to this book. To a certain extent they were conned into helping. The author appreciates it and takes this opportunity to say it.

Huntington, West Virginia
August, 1978
Danny Fulks

The best teachers do not teach, neither do
they proselytize. At most they merely affirm
the existence of the way.

> Steven Goldberg
> (A paraphrase from a
> description of Bob Dylan)

Since the late sixties a revival of the activity centered
classroom has been a prevailing element in public education in
the United States. Picking up on some old ideas of Leo Tolstoy,
Frederick Froeble, Johann Pestalozzi, Jean Rousseau, A. S. Neill,
Maria Montessori, and other historical figures and relating their
ideas to the newer findings of Jean Piaget and Jerome Brumer, the
romantics in education began to complain and tell us how the
British were doing it. John Holt, George Dennison, James Herndon,
Charles Silberman, Herbert Kohl, Paul Goodman, V. R. Rogers and
other critics became well known advocates of another historical
swing through the child centered school.

In 1967, The New Republic published a series of articles
through which Joseph Featherstone brought the news about open
education and informal learning, British style, to the United
States. Apparently, after World War II, many of the teachers in
the British Infant Schools were forced to hold classes in make-
shift facilities as a result of the destruction caused by bombs
during World War II. This situation seemed to foster the natural
autonomy of teachers in a country where democracy in the bureau-
craticic systems is given considerable attention. There were at
least two other major factors in the development of informal
learning in Britain. The findings of the Swiss developmental
psychologist, Jean Piaget, were available to lend theoretical
support; and the movement was legitimized by being accepted and
supported by the Ministry of Education.

In the British Infant Schools the children seemed to be
learning by first hand experiences through a variety of activities rather than through rigid academic disciplines and prescribed group practices so common in most elementary schools.
These kids were doing individual projects which included anything

From "Bob Dylan and the Poetry of Salvation," by Steven Goldberg,
Saturday Review, May 30, 1970, and reprinted with their permission.

from gathering hen eggs to cardboard carpentry. After a significant personal experience, the children were directed into learning activities in the accepted disciplines and skills by teachers who no longer taught in the classic sense but seemed to be more of a facilitator, a coordinator, a helper, a friend, or something that no one has been able to name with any satisfaction. Phrases such as, "the integrated day", "multi-age" or "family grouping", "learning centers", "Wendy houses", and "informal learning" became a part of the new educational jargon.

The news was well received in the United States. Americans were still smarting from the overt academic stress suffered in schools in the United States after Sputnik, Hymen Rickover, and Max Rafferty. So there were many parents, teachers, administrators, teacher educators, and probably even some children who were ready to have another go with a trend which looked similar to what some people thought was progressive education resurrected. The writers and the advocates wasted no time in finding another bandstand from which to operate.

The movement in the United States toward the open classroom complemented the times. The significant stresses and strains of the larger social system, rioting, looting, and a general harassment of the respectables were replaced by blue grass festivals, soft drugs, sex, and wine. The young people were taking a closer look at themselves and there was an underlying trend toward the consideration of simpler ways of life. The American political system was still together but there was an overwhelming distrust which was, in the early seventies, the rudiments of a visionary hunch about things to come. It was as though the radical imagination sensed that the thing was going to fall apart anyway. All they had to do was sit around and wait.

The rationale which supported informal learning was based upon conservative principles. While the movement appeared to some people to be inspired by radical heretics, a closer look at the philosophy showed its relationship to ideals which have historically been a part of the American system. Beliefs such as local autonomy, democracy in the Jeffersonian ideal, group cohesion, the willingness to help others, responsibility for one's decisions, and community spirit are not new to the American system. The one room rural schools were, in fact, often operated within the framework of these values.

If informal learning and teaching is appreciably different from traditional learning and teaching, the differences encompass two major areas, the psychological and the physical. The psychological factors which deal with human interaction aspects, values, and teaching methodology are the most difficult to describe or conceptualize. The nebulous characteristics of informal learning, however, give activity classrooms their value and essence.

Purists in the movement argue that informal learning defies quantification, that it still belongs more in the domain of poets, artists, and philosophers. It would take a writer who wrote in the manner of the late James Jones to describe informal learning. Here he describes the melody of a guitar.

> But when it came to describing for them who
> had never heard it the poignant fleeting ex-
> quisitely delicate melody of that guitar,
> memory always faltered. There was no way to
> describe them that. You had to hear that,
> the steady, swinging, never wavering beat
> with two- or three-chord haunting minor riffs
> at the end of phrases, each containing the
> whole feel and pattern of the joyously un-
> happy tragedy of this earth (and of that
> other earth). And always over it all the
> one picked single string of the melody fol-
> lowing infallibly the beat, weaving in and
> out around it with the hard-driven swiftly-
> run arpeggios, always moving, never hesita-
> ting, never getting lost and having to pause
> to get back on, shifting suddenly from the
> set light-accent of the melancholy jazz beat
> to the sharp erratic-explosive gypsy rhythm
> that cried over life while laughing at it,
> too fast for the ear to follow, too original
> for the mind to anticipate, too intricate for
> the memory to remember. Andy was not a jazz-
> man, but Andy knew guitars. The American
> Eddy Lang was good, but Django the Frenchman
> was untouchable, like God.

As teacher and pupil evaluation techniques become more refined, however, perhaps its positive and negative psychological effects on teachers and children will finally be measured to some extent.

The psychological and philosophical rationale of informal learning leads to a variety of teaching/learning practices. Forced competition among the children is eliminated. Children still compete in many ways, but they are not forced into situations where they can never win. Observers have found that children, when left alone in free play, soon stop playing games in which they are not successful. In traditional classrooms, children are normed, grouped, graded, sorted, classified, and labeled into predetermined courses of study which include social and psycho-

From Here to Eternity by James Jones. Copyright 1951 by Charles Scribner's Sons and reprinted with their permission.

logical relationships. In informal classrooms the child chooses all of his areas of competition including the academic skills, and he is compared only with his own best efforts, except in those areas where he wants to enter into the competition. The teacher guides and attempts to provide experiences to motivate, but force is unacceptable. The teacher must, moreover, promote a wide range of values within which a child can be accepted because he has learned where the wild berries grow with the kind of enthusiasm usually reserved for more conventional knowledge, such as, the Dolch list of nice words to know.

In informal classrooms there is a major concern for living today rather than preparing to live sometime in the future. The teacher and the pupils base their plans upon the belief that a series of productive days, sometimes called a school year, will be sufficient. Children prepare for adult thinking and behaving by being children rather than by playing adults. The feelings, thoughts, ideas, and information received by the teacher from the children are accepted without reservation. This type of methodology does not necessarily mean that one feeling or one piece of information is not better than another. It means that the initial encounter between the child and the teacher should be one of trust and acceptance. It means that the teacher and child will not become adversaries with the teacher consistently having correct information and good values while the child often has incorrect information and questionable values. The teacher and the child are partners, learning from one another. If the child says, "I ain't got no money", the teacher accepts the statement and may make a mental or written note concerning its quality. Later, the teacher would probably want to direct the child in learning to repeat the phrase in standard English. The teacher would not tell the child, however, that his language was unacceptable beyond his native habitat.

There is no punishment in informal classrooms. Although there are many variables of the process, William Glasser's reality therapy suggests that only sanctions be used by teachers in their efforts to control children. He defines sanctions as rules which are discussed and agreed upon by the teacher and the children. An example of a sanction is that if a child gets into a fight, he will be sent to the principal's office or some other place away from his group for a period of time. It is a very simple rule and each child is aware of the rule. The child is not punished with the infliction of physical pain or through the withdrawal of love. While he is away from the group he can work on his contracts, play quiet games, or do whatever he wants to do as long as he does not greatly disturb others who may be in the area. Most children find that it is more fun to be with their own group.

There is no propaganda in informal classrooms. Practices, procedures, processes, and ideas are accepted on merit rather than having the teacher attempt to indoctrinate children into a system of pre-determined beliefs and values. If one book is better to read than another, this will be shown by the fact that more children seem to enjoy it. If the food served in the school cafeteria does not taste good, the teacher will feel free to say, "Well, to tell you the truth, I didn't like it too well myself." It can be admitted that some people have personal and material success although they can hardly read at all. Values are promoted through example. If the teacher wants a display of good manners, whatever this means, a personal example by the teacher should be sufficient. A teacher who feels that children should take turns at the drinking fountain will follow this system along with the children. The basic idea is that children can be trusted to learn the best practices and values for them without indoctrination or other processes which imply a blind faith in authority figures.

A broad concept of freedom is permitted in informal classrooms. Children are encouraged to make choices from a variety of activities. A child can choose, for example, to go to the social studies center as soon as the day begins. In the social studies center, the child can choose from a selection of information and projects which have been arranged by the teacher. The child can also select and test different ways of learning or gaining information. Whatever the decision, the child is responsible for his choices and must practice acceptance of the responsibility that ought to be a natural part of choosing.

Informal classrooms place value on the caring aspect of human relationships. Children are accepted as they are by the teachers, and if nothing more, a personal example is provided which enables the human capabilities of caring, courage, and understanding to develop in a positive way. The teacher accepts the responsibility for being a person who can extend concern and feeling to children. The teacher gains authority on the basis of experience and competence rather than on legitimatized authority which may use fear as a basis for domination. These are human conditions which promote creativity, joy, competence, and a positive self-image for children. Children come first and the group rules which characterize many classrooms are of secondary importance.

It has been awhile since public education began in the United States. Around 1635, the first grammar school was established in the Massachusetts Bay Colony. Since that time, three-hundred years and more, some physical changes have taken place in elementary classrooms: the children have been grouped according to age and placed in separate boxes called self-contained classrooms; several classrooms have been placed within one building; electricity, central heating, and other basic utilities have been added; restrooms have been moved indoors; hot lunches have replaced cold biscuits in most schools; blackboards have gone green. In scattered areas, such ammenities as carpeting, classroom lavatories, air conditioning, modern lighting, lounge areas, and cold drinking water have been made available in schools.

There are still, however, thousands of classrooms in the United States, both old and new, which retain the basic elements of antiquated grammar schools. Giving no consideration to the significance of the nonverbal messages which children receive from their physical environment, the symbols of large group instruction remain. While the professors and publishers preach about the values of "individualized instruction", they ignore the fact that the classroom itself and many of its accouterments were designed to complement large group instruction. Consider these physical symbols which send nonverbal messages to children.

The bulletin board. It is often the only place for the display of materials or messages. It is large enough to be seen and possibly read from anywhere in the room. It often contains a seasonal display done entirely by the teacher.

The alphabet above the chalkboard. The large cursive and manuscript letters are placed at the front of the room, high on the wall, going from A to Z, assuming that all the children are facing the front.

Slant top desks facing toward the front of the classroom. The most common type of school desk found in the United States is the individual slant-top desk. It facilitates large group instruction because it precludes communication among children and only the most imaginative teacher can utilize these desks to promote individual learning.

Large chalkboards. The large chalkboard facing the class and sometimes extended to other wall space was specifically designed so the entire group could see what the teacher had written on the board.

The teacher's desk. This is a symbol of authority in the classroom. The teacher sits behind a large desk, decorates it with a fake antique brass bell, and fills the drawers with permanent records, I. Q. scores, and other intimidating information. The desk often contains a paddle and the teacher's personal effects. The message to the children is that they should keep away from this object.

The window locations. Elementary classrooms almost invariably have a long row of windows placed so the light can enter and project over the left shoulders of the children. This means that they must all face the same direction.

Thirty copies of the same book title. Textbook publishers argue that every child must have a copy of the same book at the same time. This idea is explicit for large group instruction. If the school program is for individuals, there is no need for more than six or seven copies of any given book.

Sterile walls, ceiling, floors, and other forms of austerity. Ancient philosophers and learning theoreticians believed that children were easily distracted by such things as colorful walls, pictures, and objects outside the classroom window. These physical factors were, therefore, kept drab so that children would concentrate on their lessons.

Audio-visual equipment. Most classrooms have been equipped with large screens for film viewing, overhead projectors, 23 inch television sets, and other pieces of equipment. This type of equipment was designated for large group instruction and, therefore, if used according to operating instructions or tradition, will inhibit individual learning.

Classrooms for elementary students must be physically changed to accommodate the assumptions which undergird informal learning. In fact, there are many educators and even a few of the old timers down on the courthouse square who believe that classrooms for children should resemble a poor man's Disney World. They should be colorful and attractive to children; the ceilings should be lowered, if not actually, at least with homemade mobiles; children can learn to read surrounded by plastic alligators and red-eyed ducks; they can learn math on a mezzanine built for five; they can develop their oral language while they make themselves comfortable on a (fireproof) rug. So it goes, an age old philosophy with the basic premise that children develop best by being children. Given the proper psychological and physical environment, a minimum of direct intervention by adults is adequate.

Adjustments in teacher orientation, however, are not easy. Among the factors that inhibit significant change in teacher behavior are such institutional factors as building and equipment design, administrative policy, peer pressure, and the orientation of tradition. The community at large is also a contributing factor. Rising above all of these variables, though, is the teacher.

Teachers, like all members of the human race, have deeply rooted attitudes and values that have been internalized through their individual experiences. These attitudes and values, however covert, can be converted into assumptions about children and the way they learn. Teachers who find the following assumptions acceptable will have little difficulty with informal learning. Teachers who cannot accept a substantial number of them will have to take a look at themselves and attempt a personal evaluation of their beliefs before they can direct an informal classroom.

Assumptions

1. Children learn through play.
2. Children learn to trust by being trusted.
3. Children learn from each other.
4. Children learn best when they are content.
5. The best way for children to learn about democracy is to practice it through decision making.
6. Children should have the opportunity to exercise choice in their learning pursuits.
7. Children should practice learning what to do when they don't know what to do.
8. There is no discrete body of knowledge that every child needs to learn.
9. Children are more important than content.
10. Children should not be grouped arbitrarily in any manner that could diminish their self concept.
11. Discipline problems are diminished when children are engaged in activities of their own interest.
12. Children should compete with their own best efforts rather than with other children.
13. Failure and other forms of rejection should be removed from all learning situations.
14. The best learning occurs when children are active in the learning process.
15. The primary purpose of a classroom should be to help children learn to think.
16. Children will investigate a vital environment without external coercion or reward.
17. The highest form of knowing is acquired through nonverbal processes.
18. Learning strategies should be completely individualized.
19. Children progress at their own pace through developmental stages at a rate peculiar to each child.
20. Structure should be developed in the environment coupled with each child's experience base rather than on external authority.
21. Children should be provided maximum opportunities to help one another.
22. Children should be involved directly in experiences and activities prior to instruction.
23. Children must be accepted as they are.

These are merely assumptions. This means that any of them are open for further argument and speculation. No one really knows whether they are true. It is probably reasonable to state

that some of them are true for some children some of the time when
certain human and physical variables are present and active.

WHAT IS A LEARNING CENTER?

Most traditional school classroom designs have failed to meet the physical and psychological needs of children. With designs based on antiquated assumptions about how children learn, the physical attributes of traditional classrooms seem to accommodate adults more than they do the children they were meant to serve. Austerity has been a byword with sterile walls, high ceilings, hard floors, and hard seats. Yet, this physical matter that is supposed to be a learning environment communicates significant messages to the children. The lack of areas for privacy tells children that they are not trusted. The hard seats that children are forced to sit in for long hours communicate the message that learning is mental and physical discipline, and hard work. The austere nature of the classroom itself tells children that education is not really as important as commerce when contrasted with new car showrooms that are carpeted and enclosed in plate glass.

Drastic changes in classroom design and physical format are not easily effected. Teachers who accept the assumptions stated in Chapter One can, however, make many accommodations which will result in environmental improvements. While these factors may appear to some to be short on intellectualism, the underlying rationale for a vital learning environment is substantiated by significant educational philosophers and theoreticians.

The physical characteristics of learning centers may be described as follows:

Learning centers are semiprivate areas set apart from the remaining classroom space.

Learning centers are normally identified with a given disciplinary stress--language, math, fine arts, social studies, the sciences, or a nondescript area for miscellaneous activities.

Learning centers are designed to facilitate the physical aspects of a learning environment for children or adolescents. The matter that is placed in the centers should essentially represent the academic discipline for which the center is designed. The physical matter should be placed within easy reach of the children and it should be stored in boxes, sacks, plastic bags or other types of containers to help keep the center stuff organized. Shelves, drawers, desk tops, and other holding equipment are also helpful. Containers for file folders, card files, books, diaries, and related matter are important for space utilization and neatness.

Learning centers should be warm and cozy, naturally alive, and attractive to children. The children are afforded some privacy and trust. A variety of arrangements should be available so that the children may stand, sit, or lie on the floor, or sit on chairs or benches. A fireproof rug or carpet should be used to cover the center floor area.

Learning centers might be described as sophisticated play houses. Children will build play houses from furniture and other objects when they are placed in a large room and are provided with building materials. This is the way children convert a physical environment to structures that better fit their own sizes. Learning centers represent, among other things, an accommodation to this seldom recognized need among children.

The most practical way to change traditional classroom design, physical format, and furnishings is for the teachers to do it themselves. Waiting for a new building, a new shipment of furniture, or a hundred boxes of commercial materials from the exclusive supply houses is a tedious process. The PTA may come through with twenty-five dollars or one might rip off a cafeteria table. Basically, however, teachers are on their own and must make do with their own resources. This is not an altogether negative situation. Those teachers who have developed the ability and initiative to reconstruct their teaching areas through the use of cheap materials and junk are likely to be more autonomous, therefore less likely to rely on authority figures in institutions for direction.

To begin the process of implementing learning centers in a traditional classroom, the furniture, equipment, and materials should be arranged into some different settings. One must consider that, initially, commercial supplies which lend themselves to flexibility may not be available. It is, therefore, vital to utilize imagination in converting matter that is readily available into new schemes which are more conducive to open education.

The storage areas such as cabinets, closets, and coat rooms in many classrooms often become containers for matter which is no longer used by the teacher or the students. It is not uncommon to find faded construction paper, multiple copies of outdated textbooks, empty glue bottles, miscellaneous items of lost clothing, and et cetera cluttering up classroom storage areas. The first step for a teacher who is beginning the physical preparation for learning centers would be to clear all of the classroom storage areas, rid them of unusable matter, and, perhaps, add some color with contact paper or paint. During this process, the teacher can begin to sort and classify the junk material which was found in the storage areas. The orientation toward a different kind of methodology about matter is important to informal education and should be another initial consideration. Examples of resourcefulness in converting things which appear worthless into learning materials are: (1) Tear stories from outdated texts and make them into small paperback booklets to place in a learning center and; (2) Cut an old rubber overshoe into strips and place the strips in a center. There are, of course, a thousand other ways to utilize such matter.

The physical conversion of a traditional classroom into learning centers also demands that existing chairs, desks, bookcases, file cabinets, projector carts, and tables be utilized in different ways. A typical traditional arrangement, for example, places the students in the center of the classroom seated in rows while bookcases, cabinets, and other storage equipment is placed against the walls. This procedure should essentially be reversed for informal classrooms. Matter which is movable should be placed in box or L-shaped formations throughout the classroom. Several small areas to accommodate groups of four to six students should be built by placing the existing furniture in a manner which is conducive to privacy and comfort for the students. After the physical arrangement is changed in the preceding manner, one can observe the physical needs which remain. Perhaps a few sheets of plywood or plasterboard should be used to further the effect of privacy. Just the changes made with the existing matter, however, will have an effect on teaching and learning within the classroom. One should also consider the conversion of coat rooms, large wall cabinets, or areas adjacent to the classroom entrance door as learning centers. The author's experience has been that, especially in older buildings, many such areas are wasted as far as space utilization for students is concerned. These spaces often have more appeal to students than centers which can be built in the conventional classroom area.

In Chapter One, the author described nine physical symbols of tradition and large group instruction. Among these symbols was the austere appearance of conventional classrooms. A second phase of implementing an informal classroom is getting away from austerity and picking up on physical appearances which are attractive to students and, to a large degree, are made by the students themselves. Among some things to consider using in a different manner are conventional items such as pictures of Washington and Lincoln, large alphabet letters above the blackboard, teacher made bulletin boards, and trite pronouncements such as, "We Love to Read", "We All Brush Our Teeth", or "Spring is Here". There is nothing wrong with pictures of Washington or Lincoln, but students get bored with them after awhile and there are other worthy personalities one can consider. The ABC's above the chalkboard can be hung from the ceiling throughout the classroom as one would hang a mobile or, better yet, smaller editions of these can be placed in learning centers or on table tops. The trite pronouncements could probably be eliminated with no substantial loss to academics. Today's television child has been nutured by Madison Avenue and is often intelligent enough to know that we do not all brush our teeth, and that the appearance of spring is obvious. A phrase such as Some Children Like Books may be an improvement as far as communication is concerned.

If the best knowledge available about how children learn is plausible, a colorful classroom has a positive effect on learning and behavior. The walls should be utilized to the fullest with creative art produced by the students, augmented with items chosen by the teacher. The ceiling should at least have several mobiles attached which create a visual effect equivalent to a lower ceiling. Another consideration is to obtain containers such as shoe boxes to store the students' personal effects. By removing each child's personal materials from a given desk, the desks can be utilized in a more flexible manner. The students learn after an orientation period that they can move about the room to work and play in areas of their choice as long as they maintain an orderly procedure which is necessary for management in informal classrooms.

The ideas mentioned above are not presented as a step-by-step method for physically converting a classroom from a traditional to a more modern appearance. These ideas are meant, rather, to stimulate the reader's imagination and creativity in designing and implementing a classroom decor. They are also meant to endorse the belief that children learn better in a fun place than in a place where every piece of matter is a reminder of what we commonly call drudgery.

In an interview with Eleanor Duckworth (Learning, October, 1973), Jean Piaget said that,

> "Manipulation of materials is crucial. In order to think, children in the concrete stage need to have objects in front of them that are easy to handle, or else be able to visualize objects that have been handled and that are easily imagined without any real effort."

Piaget was really saying that children learn to think better if they have stuff to mess around with.

Piaget's belief about the significance of having a vital environment for educational purposes in the schools is incongruent with the theories of ancient educational philosophers who, under idealism and realism, believed that such an environment only served to distract students from the important things found in books or told to them by their teachers. Their philosophies, deeply entrenched in western schools, have had a major impact in causing educational practitioners to keep the learning environment sterile. A student could not, they thought, mess around with trinkets without missing out on something important. As a result of these beliefs, many students have been plunged too early into the abstractions of mathematics, language, and other academic areas. The west has, reluctantly at times, accepted nursery schools and kindergartens as places to "fool around"; but when a student entered the first grade it was time for him to settle down, get into straight rows, put away his childish toys, and begin racking up those A's and B's.

Many professional educators are familiar with the Dewian philosophy of learning by doing. John Dewey said the same thing Piaget had been saying back at the turn of the century. Many educators failed to appreciate the depth of Dewey's commitment and seemed to think that their students were learning by doing: doing arithmetic, problem after problem; doing reading at a given grade or level; and so on. In fact, the progressive education movement of the late twenties and early thirties probably failed because the teachers turned to their students and said, "Well, what do you want to do?", without providing a variety of options. In classrooms where the choices were limited to pencil and paper work, many students chose to yell at each other, turn over chairs, or create chaos in a thousand ways. So the progressive movement died a natural death, and there were few mourners.

An activity classroom must have stuff with which the kids can be active. Students cannot interact in a productive way with an environment which lacks vitality. They cannot learn through experience prior to abstraction except where there are things to experience.

In informal classrooms, an array of matter must be available for students to smell, feel, taste, hear, see, and manipulate. Everything that is safe and can be accommodated physically in a classroom should be considered. It may be necessary for teachers to scrounge materials from the farms, the streets, the garage sales, the attics, anywhere good junk can be found. In doing this, and in learning how to make an activity classroom work, teachers are achieving two goals: (1) they are becoming more autonomous as professionals and; (2) they are practicing a teaching methodology which reflects the best in contemporary theories. Consider a list of matter which was compiled by the author and teachers with whom he worked:

Abacus, acorns, add-a-count scale, adding maching, adhesive tape, alcohol, algae, Alka Seltzer bottles, almanacs, alphabet cereal, altimeter, aluminum, animal pictures, animal skeleton, animal teeth, ant farm, applebutter paddle, apple seeds, aquarium, arrows, arrow heads, artificial fingernails, Atlas, attribute games and blocks, auger and bits, autoharp, awls, axle.

Balance, balance scales, ball bearings, balloons, bamboo strips, bandaids, bark, barley, barometer, baseballs, basic shapes, basket weaving materials, bathroom scales, batteries, beads, beans, bellows, bells, berries for dying, bias tape, bicycle parts, bicycle wheel (mounted), binary counter, binoculars, biographies, bird bath, bird feeders, bird houses, bird house plans, birds' nests, blank checks (fake), bleach jugs, boatswain pipe, bobbins, bolts, bongos, bottle stoppers, bows, boxes (all sizes), brass kettle, brayer, bricks, broomstick, brushes, buckeyes, bumper stickers, burlap, butter churn, butterflies, butterfly net, buttons.

Cactus, calendars, caliper, camel saddle, camera, candle holder, candles, candy, canteen, cardboard, card file of activities, card games, carpet samples, carriage, cash register, cassette recorders, catalog cards, cellophane, ceramic tiles (small), chains, chaps, charcoal, checkers, cheese cloth, chess, chewing gum, chicken coop, chicken feed, child's hand operated sewing machine, china (old pieces), chopsticks, cigar holder, cigarette filters, cigarette packages, cigar boxes, cinder blocks, circus posters, clay, clip board, clocks, cloth (all kinds), clothespins, coal, coal bucket, coasters, coat hangers, cocoa, coconut shells, cocoons, coffee, coffee cans, coffee grinder, color cubes, comic books, commercial text (few copies), compasses, computer cards, concrete shapes and forms, construct-a-cube puzzle, construction paper, contact paper, containers for measuring liquid, cookie cutters, cookies, coonskin cap, coral, cord, cork, corn, corn cob pipe, corn cobs, corn shucks, corn silk, corrugated paper, cosmetics, cottage cheese cartons, count-a-ladder and pegs, counting bar, cow bell, cow's horn, cradle, cray fish, crayons, cribbage board, chrochet hooks, crosscut saw, crushed stone, cube puzzles (game), cubical counting blocks, cubic measuring materials, Cuisenaire cubes, Cuisenaire rods, cupcake liners, curlers, curling iron, currie combs, curtain hooks, cushions, cymbals.

Dairy feed, decals, decimal and percentage board, dehorners, derby, desk calculator, diary books, dice, dictionary, dinner bell, discarded jewelry, discarded pictures from home, distilled water, doilies, doll clothes, doll house, dolls, dominoes, door knobs, doweling, dress form, dress patterns, driftwood, drills, drinking straws, drums, dry concrete mix, dust pan, dyes.

Easel, eggs, egg shells, embroidery hoops, emery board, empty medicine containers, encyclopedias, envelopes, etching materials, extension cords, eyes scarves.

False eyelashes, feathers, felt, felt board, felt markers, felt scraps, fiberglass, file folders, film, film loop pictures, film loops, film negatives, film strips, filter paper, finger paints, fish, fish net, flags, flash cards, flashlight, flint, flip charts, floor tiles, flour, flourescent paint, flower pots, flowers, flutophone, foil, folding ruler, food coloring, foreign money, fossils, fraction discs, French harp, fruit (all kinds), funnel, Funnel's thermometer, fur.

Gallon jug, games, garden, gas mask, gauges and dials from instrument panels, geoblocks, geoboard, geometric models, geometric shapes, geometric solids, gerbils, glass, glassware, glitter, globe, glue, gold prospecting equipment, golf balls, golf tees, gourds, grapes, graphite, graph paper, grass, grasshoppers, gravel, grease pencils, grocery store items, gum erasers, gummed paper.

Hair of goat, horse, and cow, hammer, hand operated tire pump, hand organ, hand tools, hardback story books, hard tack, harmonica, harness, hats (all kinds), hay, head dress, hem tape, hickory nuts, hinges, hole puncher, holly, honeycomb, hoops, hornets' nests, horns of cow, deer, and goat, horse bridle, horse muzzle, horseshoes, hot plate, hour glass, house plans.

Ice cream freezer, ice cream sticks, index box, Indian blanket, Indian corn, ink pad, inner-tubes, insect catcher.

Jacks, jug-saw puzzle, junk mail.

Keys and locks, kegs, kiln, kitchen utensils, kites, knitting needles.

Labels from cans and boxes, lace, lantern, lead, lead from bullets, leather goods, leaves, lever, lichens, light bulbs, liquid measuring material, liquid soap, litmus paper, live animals and insects, loose leaf rings, love beads, lumber.

Magazines, magic slates, magnetic board, magnets, magnifying glass, mail order catalogs, maps, maracas, marble chips, marbles, match boxes, matching cubes, material pieces, math bingo, math records, meal measuring wheel, mechanical puzzles, medicine dropper, megaphone, menus, meter sticks, Mexican jumping beans, micrometer caliper, military insignia, milk cartons, milkers, milking stool, mirrors, mistletoe, moccasins, model animals, model cars, model soldiers, molded bread, money, mop, moss, moth balls, mud, multibase blocks, mushrooms, mustache wax.

Nail polish, nails, Napier's rods, newspaper, number lines, number rays, nuts, nylon stockings.

Oatmeal boxes, odd and even number cards, odometer, old bifocals, old calendars, old campaign buttons, old Christmas cards, old clocks, old clothes, old ledger, old medicine bottles, old parasals, old radios, old school bell, old school slates, old shoes, old stamps, old telephone, old television set parts, old Woody Guthrie records, orange juice cans, orange seeds, order forms from catalogs.

Paints, pans, paper (various kinds), paper bags, paper clips, paper cups, paper-mache, paper plates, paper tissue flowers, paper towels, paperback books, parts of automobiles, paste, patterns for making the Five Basic Polyhedra, peanuts, pear seads, pecans, peck basket, pegs, peg boards, pencils, pens, perfume, perimeter area boards, persimmons, phrasestrips, piano, pi circle, picture frames, pictures, pictures of musical instruments, pin cushions, pineapples, pine cones, pine needles, ping pong balls, pinking shears, pins, pipe cleaners, pitcher and wash bowl, pitch pipe, place value holder, place value sticks, plaster of Paris, plastic animals, plastic bags, plastic bottles, plastic buckets, plastic flowers and fruit, plastic screen, plastic tape, playing cards, pliers, plow, plumbing and joints, plywood, pocketbooks, poker chips, pond water, pop bottle caps, popcorn, popsicle sticks, portable organ, poster paper, posters, potholders, powder horn, prime number board, printing press, prism, projectors, protractors, pulleys, pumpkin, puppets, putty.

Q-tips, quart basket, quilting frame.

Raisins, raw potatoes, raw tobacco, recipes, record albums, record player, rhubarb, ribbon, rice, rickrack, road maps, road signs, rock candy, rock salt, rocking chairs, Roman numeral kit, rope, rubber balls, rubber bands, rubber cement, rubber stamps, rubber worms, rugs, rulers.

Saddle bags, salamanders, salt, sand, sandpaper, sassafras, saw, sawdust, scales, scissors, scrap paper, screwdriver, screws, seagrass string, seam gauge, sea shells, seeds (all kinds), self-made story books, sequence picture cards, sequins, sets, sets for finding Cartesian products, shape tracers, shark teeth, shaving cream, shellac, shepherd's staff, shirt cards, shoe boxes, shoe polish, shoestring, shot from empty shot gun shells, shuck beans, side saddle, sieve, silverware, simple machines, shrunken heads, slide ruler, small chalk board, small rocks (all forms), snake skin, snuff box, soap, socks, soda, soda straws, soft drink mix, soil (all forms), solid geometric shapes, soybeans, spats, spices, spinning wheel, sponges, spools, spoons (musical), spray paint, springs, spurs, squash, stage make-up, stamps, stapler, staple remover, staples, steel wool pads, step-bells, stethoscope, stop watch, stove pipe hat, straw, straw hat, string, stuffed animals, stylus, styrofoam, suction cups, sum-stick, sunglasses, super-market advertisements, sweet potatoes.

Tadpoles, tambourine, tanagrams, tape measure, tape player, tape recorder, tapes, tea, telephone directory, tennis racket, terrarium, test tubes, thermometer, thimble, thread spools, thumb tacks, timers, tinsel, tissue paper, tissues, toadstools, toilet paper tubes, tongs, tomahawks, tongue depressors, toothpicks, totem pole, Towers of Hanoi (game), toy money, toys, tracing wheel, transparent cubes, travel folders, travois, trundle, trunk, Tuf (game), tuning fork, tweezers, typewriter.

Ukulele.

Varnish, vase, vegetables, vinegar, Vinn diagram hoops.

Walnuts, washboard, washers, wasp nests, water bucket, wax wax paper, weekly thermometer chart, weights (avoirdupois and metric), wheels, wheat, wheat paste, whistles, wigs, willow branches for horns, Will Rogers records, wire (all forms), wire cutter, wire geometric forms and patterns, wood (all kinds), wood and metal files, wood flats, wood scraps, wooden dowel rods (varying sizes), wooden shoes, word builder box, words and alphabet cards, wrenches.

Yardsticks, yarn, yeast.

Zither.

Content and skill from the disciplines of language arts, the sciences, fine arts, mathematics, and social studies are not separated in the minds of children. They are only separated for the convenience of daily classroom programming, textbook producers, curriculum guides, evaluation, and the principal's file cabinet. It is, in fact, impossible to learn about any of these traditional disciplines apart from all the others. However, the establishment of effective learning centers should be done with a particular disciplinary stress--the word stress is used in an attempt to clarify the assumption that a discrete separation is not merely impossible--it is an unacceptable way to organize for learning. Children probably do not think in terms of mathematics separated from language or art.

In order to stress a given discipline, the matter that is placed in a learning center must reflect this stress. The matter does not attempt to separate--it emphasizes. Taking the five major disciplines and assuming that the physical space is ready, one might consider the partial list of matter presented below to emphasize each discipline.

Language Arts: almanacs, alphabet cereal, boxes for puppet stage, brochures, bulletin board, camera, camera film, carpet, catalogs, chalk, cigar boxes, comic books, crayons, crossword puzzles, diary books, encyclopedia, felt markers, file folders, food coloring, gerbils, gummed paper, index activity box, junk mail, labels from cans, magazines, menus, mirror, newspapers, old stories, pencils, phrase strips, pictures, pineapple, poetry books, puppets, puzzles, record player, records, road signs, sandpaper letters, self-made story books, small chalk board, soap carvings, spelling thesaurus, straw, tags, telephone directory, typewriter, weekly readers.

Fine Arts: autoharp, balloons, bells, brushes, buttons, cardboard, castonets, cellophane, chalk, clay, contact paper, crayons, drinking straws, easel, egg cartons, etching materials, feathers, food coloring, glitter, glue, harmonica, leather goods, mud, newspaper, paints, paper bags, paper-mache, paper towels, pipe cleaners, puppets and stage, rickrack, rocks, sand, scissors, seeds, sequins, spoons, sponge, string, tissue paper, ukulele, wax, weaving material whistle, wire, woodblock, xylophone, yarn.

Mathematics: abacus, acorns, attribute game, basic shapes, bathroom scales, beans, caliper, chalk, checkbook, cigar boxes, clocks, clothespins, color cubes, color pegs and boards, compass, Cuisenaire rods, dice, dominoes, geoblocks, geoboards, golf tees, graph paper, grocery store items, hickory nuts, homemade balance, instrument panels, jacks, kitchen scales, marbles, measuring containers, Napier's rods, number line, play money, poleidoblocks, popsicle sticks, rocks for counting, rulers, shape tracers, slide rule, spools, springs, stop watch, styrofoam blocks, tanagram, thermometer, transparent cubes, washers, water, wheels.

Social Studies: almanac, Atlas, binoculars, branding irons, brochures, bull ring, butter churn, camera, camera film, candles, charts, circus posters, coconut, coffee grinder, cotton, dictionary, fish net, flags, foods from other climates, globe, grass skirt, hats, historical painting, hooked rugs, Indian corn, Indian relics, Indian wigwam, maps, Mexican jumping beans, native costumes, newspapers, old campaign buttons, old telephone, peanuts, pictures, pineapple, pottery, powder horn, quilt, slides, soap, soldier's uniform, stamp collection, tobacco seeds, travel posters, washboard, wooden shoes.

Science: ant farm, aquarium, balloons, barometer, batteries, bird's nest, bricks, cactus, camera, camera film, candles, cocoons, daily weather chart, empty medicine bottles, feathers, filter paper, flower pot, food coloring, funnels, gerbils, hay, honeycomb, hornets' nest, inner tubes, light bulbs, litmus paper, magnetic board, magnifying glass, mirror, paperback books, paraffin, prisms, raw tobacco, rocks, rope, salt, sand, screws, seeds, soap, stethoscope, straw, sugar, terrarium, vinegar, water.

CURRICULUM PLANNING FOR THE INTEGRATED DAY

The phrase, integrated day, is another piece of educational jargon from the British Isles. To integrate a program of studies for a group of children or adolescents means that there is no attempt to separate the school day into discrete time periods for mathematics, language arts, or other curriculum areas. It is assumed that students are constantly learning as individuals from all disciplines at any given time. In order to facilitate this phenomena of human learning, curriculum projects which encompass several subjects should be devised by teachers in cooperation with their students. This is a step beyond "correlation", a word widely used in the fifties to describe teaching methods in which two disciplines were tangled together.

The author asked graduate students in elementary education to develop curriculum projects which show the integration of subject matter. The students were to: (1) Begin a specific activity with a small group. No instruction was to be given prior to the activity; (2) Show how material from each curriculum area can be learned in relation to this initial activity; (3) Develop for each curriculum area a list of inquiry and fact oriented questions and an extensive vocabulary list; (4) Show how the content expands into a never ending array of data which could be described as an upside-down pyramid with the top indicating that knowledge is expanding rather than closing. The project was not closed or "culminated"; it was left open. A name for the project might be "Jerome Bruner after taxes" because it represents discovery in a simple format.

Two examples of curriculum projects based upon this inquiry rationale follow. The first, developed by Jo Ann Gainer, began with a field trip to Cherry River Falls in Nicholas County, West Virginia. The second project, by Rebecca Burris, began with an activity using tin cans.

EXPLORING CHERRY RIVER FALLS   Jo Ann Gainer

This experimental learning experience took place on an early September afternoon, at the falls of the Cherry River. The Monongahela National Forest encloses the river on both sides and the leaves of the forest trees were beginning to change color. The river is not wide at this point, and a three foot high stone wall extends across to make the falls. Below the falls are "the rocks" where many young couples go exploring on summer evenings. The water level is low and the water lazily rolls over the falls and tumbles down among the rocks into the deepest area. Most of the rocks are dry. Many traces remain of earlier summer inhabitants.

After lunch, about twenty second graders and I hiked to the falls to find out about anything and everything. A short narrow path led us to the spot. The children were doing something they loved to do--EXPLORE; on the bank, along the edges of the water, across the wall of the falls, on top and between the rocks, through the shallow streams, and in the swimming hole.

SCIENCE

Activities/
Questions:

1. Make a wildlife aquarium and/or terrarium using many different things that live and grow at the falls.
2. Lead a clean up campaign.
3. Collect, observe, and experiment with samples of river water from different areas of the falls.
4. Find out what animals and plants live and grow in and around the falls.
5. What is wildlife? Why are they called wildlife? Of what is air made? How is air purified over the falls?
6. Can you smell the air? Taste it? Does air smell different in different places? Can you name some places where the air smells different? Why does it smell different and what does it smell like?
7. Do you know the difference between rocks, stones, pebbles, gravel, and sand? How do they look different? Do they feel different?
8. What things are stones used in making? Pebbles? Gravel? Sand?
9. How did we make drainage for soil, plants, and moss in the terrarium? Why is drainage necessary?
10. Of what is water made? How does it feel? How does it smell and taste?
11. Can you freeze water? Will frozen water melt? Will water boil? Find out.
12. What do we get from water for our growing bodies?
13. Why do plants, animals, and people need water?
14. What is added to drinking water to take care of our teeth? Can you taste or smell it?
15. What does moisture feel like? Can you see it?
16. What does dampness feel like? Is there a difference between moisture and dampness?
17. What do plants need to live and grow? Where do plants get their food?
18. What is ecology? Why should be learn about ecology?

19. What is air pollution? What does pollution do to plants, animals, and people?
20. What kinds of pollution do you see? Why should we not litter? What other kinds of pollution have you seen before?
21. Why do we need forests? For what is timber used?
22. How did the Snowshoe rabbit get his name?
23. With what is a river stocked? How is it stocked? From where do the fish come?
24. Can you name two kinds of fish found in the Cherry River?
25. What are minnows? For what are minnows used?
26. How does a hatchery raise so many fish?
27. How do fish breathe? What do fish eat?
28. Describe what moss looks like. What is moss? What does it feel like? Where does moss grow?
29. Name five plants that grow in the woods.
30. Name five animals that live in the forest.
31. Can fish live out of the water? Why or why not?
32. Do insects live in and out of the water?
33. What is the difference between a river, a stream, and a pond?
34. What is a current? Can you see it? Can you feel it?
35. Where do frogs live? Do frogs like waterfalls? Why or why not?
36. Make some mudpies in small tin cans. Let them dry out. What changes did you see after they dried from when you first made them? Where did the water in the mud go?

Vocabulary:

wildlife	hydrogen	oxygen
carbon dioxide	serated	rocks
stones	pebbles	gravel
sand	drainage	terrarium
aquarium	moss	freeze
melt	boil	minerals
vitamins	flourine	moisture
dampness	ecology	pollution
litter	timber	Snowshoe rabbit
stock	hatchery	golden fish
rainbow fish	minnows	bait
insects	current	river
stream	pond	evaporate
sugar maple	pine	spruce
experiment	breathe	snakes
poisonous	non-poisonous	groundhogs
collection	observe	campaign

soil	ferns	environment
prevent	restore	organisms
sediment	particles	poison ivy
rhododendren	mountain laurel	fresh water
stagnant	cardinal	gills

MATHEMATICS

Activities/
Questions:

1. Collect several stones of different sizes and shapes. Count them, put them in sets, combine and separate them.
2. Use the stones as counters in working addition and subtraction problems.
3. Compare the stones. Which one is the largest? Smallest? Flatest? Smoothest? Roughest? Heaviest? Lightest?
4. Can you arrange your stones in sets of 8's? 5's? 2's? Even numbered sets?
5. How many more stones or less stones do you have than a friend in class?
6. Who collected the most stones in class? Check your answer with a friend's.
7. How many trees do you think are growing in the forest? Can you count more than 100?
8. How many fallen trees can you count? Why do you suppose they fell?
9. Count the petals on some wild flowers.
10. How many petals have most of the flowers?
11. Can you find any flowers that have an even number of petals? What do you know about flowers and the number of petals they have?
12. How deep is the water? Use a yardstick to measure depth in different areas of the swimming hole. Is the water shallow or deep?
13. Use a yardstick to measure the height of the fall wall in inches. How many inches wide is the wall?
14. Estimate the length of a minnow in inches. Looking at a ruler will help you.
15. Make two mudballs equal in size. What shape are they? Flatten one into a pancake shape. Which one weighs the most?
16. Find a stick or any other median to draw shapes in the sand. Draw a circle, triangle, square, semi-circle, rectangle, a five-sided figure, a nine-sided figure.
17. Write down what time we leave the falls. Write down what time we get back to school. Can you figure out how long it takes to walk back to

36

school? Does it take about the same amount of
time to come back as it did to get there?
18. Count all the things you see that need water to
live and grow.
19. Is your house or the school closer to the Cherry
River Falls? How do you know?

Vocabulary:

size	shapes	combine
sets	separate	count
addition	subtraction	compare
large	small	flat
smooth	rough	heavy
light	arrange	even
add	more	less
check	petals	depth
deep	shallow	area
yardstick	inches	feet
yard	high	low
measure	wide	estimate
narrow	ruler	equal
weigh	median	circle
triangle	square	semi-circle
rectangle	figure	time
amount	equal	arithmetic

SOCIAL STUDIES

Activities/
Questions:

1. Make a salt map on heavy corrugated cardboard
showing the north fork, south fork, and the con-
fluence of the Cherry River. Mark the Cherry
River Falls and Richwood on your map.
2. Using a West Virginia map, find out what four
rivers combine with the Cherry River to form an
even larger river. What is the name of the
larger river they form?
3. Where does the Cherry River originate? Name
the mountain and falls located there.
4. What kind of fish do we catch in West Virginia?
Name five.
5. How do the coal mines pollute our rivers?
What chemical do they deposit in the rivers?
What color does the water turn?
6. What is the difference between fishermen and
hunters?
7. What animals live in the Monongahela National
Forest?
8. What is game? What game are hunters licensed
to hunt? How old must you be to get a hunting

37

or fishing license? How much does it cost?
For what is the fee used?

9. What are natural resources? What are our leading natural resources in West Virginia?

10. What are some things the Department of Natural
Resources does for our state?

11. What is our state motto? What does it mean?

12. What is the difference between a hillbilly and
a mountaineer?

13. Visit the Gauley Ranger Station.

14. From where does our drinking water in Richwood
come?

15. What occasion in Richwood derived its name from
the Cherry River? When does it take place?

16. What falls have you been to in West Virginia?

17. In what mountain range is West Virginia cen-
trally located?

18. What is our state bird, state flower, and state
tree? Did you see them today?

19. Is the Monongahela National Forest a hard wood
forest or a soft wood forest? What does
national mean?

20. Find some examples of hard wood trees and soft
wood trees in our area.

21. How do most of the people in Richwood earn a
living? Name three additional occupations of
people in Richwood.

22. What are some things done by the forestry
service?

23. Bring in a forest ranger, coal miner, or game
warden to talk to the children and answer
questions.

Vocabulary:

salt map	corrugated	cardboard
confluence	map	form
Kennison Mountain	Hill's Creek Falls	pollute
chemical	deposit	orange
fishermen	hunters	game
license	fee	Gauley
hillbilly	mountaineer	coal miner
ranger	station	Appalachian
festival	August	Mountains
hard wood	soft wood	national
examples	area	warden
originate	Bass	Muskies
catfish	Bluegill	Rainbow
occasion	sand	gravel
stone	natural gas	coal
wild turkey	wildcats	black bear
deer	sulfur	cardinal
sugar maple	rhododendron	Monongahela
forestry	natural resources	

FINE ARTS

Activities/
Questions:

1. Make a collage about what we explored today. Use pictures from <u>Wonderful West Virginia</u>, old magazines, newspapers, and other materials you choose.
2. Draw a picture using the colors you saw while exploring. Can you name all the colors you used? Did you blend some of the colors together?
3. Pretend you are a waterfall. Show me what you look like using water colors, finger paints, or crayons.
4. Make a mobile using some of the things you found today.
5. What color is the river? What colors are the rocks, trees, and wildlife? Draw or paint a picture using all of these colors.
6. Dramatize a story the class makes up that takes place at the falls.
7. While listening to music, draw a picture of what the music reminds you about our trip.
8. Squish your feet around in the mud. How does it feel? Now make footprints on the rocks or on construction paper. Look at your footprints.
9. Collect some large sticks or pieces of wood while exploring. Use a penknife to carve different shapes, or use tempera to paint designs on the wood. What have you made?
10. Gather several stones to paint. Do your own thing with the paint brush.
11. Find an object while exploring and dip it into paint. Cover an entire sheet of paper by printing designs with your object.
12. Gather long stemmed wild flowers and make a necklace or bracelet flower chain.
13. Find a pretty stone. Knot a leather shoestring several times around the stone to make a necklace. What could you call this?
14. Show filmstrips or slides of West Virginia, nature and wildlife.
15. Collect several pine cones. Cut off the bottoms to make a flat surface. Mount them upright with glue on corrugated cardboard. Snowflock for the effect of a snow covered forest.
16. On what kind of tree do pine cones grow? What other trees have cones?
17. Make mudpies or other shapes out of mud. Make designs in your objects. Let them dry in the sun.

18. Sing "Row, Row, Row Your Boat" in rounds.
19. Listen to the sounds around us. Can you sing one note on the same pitch as a sound you hear?
20. Look at the colors around you. Are there different shades of color in nature? Do you think nature is pretty or ugly? Why?
21. Learn to sing "Way Down Upon the Swannee River" and other songs about rivers. Where is the Swannee River?
22. Listen to several selections of music. Think about nature and of what the music reminds you.

Vocabulary:

collage	materials	colors
blend	pretend	mobile
draw	paint	dramatize
construction	art	music
squish	prints	carve
shapes	designs	tempera
flower chain	knot	leather
flat	surface	cones
glue	snowflock	sing
pitch	note	Swannee River
film strips	slides	rounds
object	mount	cardboard
create	selection	nature

PHYSICAL EDUCATION

Activities/
Questions:

1. Tape the sounds of the falls. Have the children create movements to the sounds.
2. Let's have a mudball battle. How does it feel to get hit by a mudball? Practice throwing so you can hit your enemy just about every time. Use strategy.
3. Try to dodge every mudball. Can you make it through the battle without getting hit?
4. In the shallow part of the swimming hole practice bobbing and rhythmic breathing. Can you bob five consecutive times? Ten?
5. Show me how a snake would crawl over the rocks. How would a grasshopper move? A turtle? A bobcat?
6. Listening to music, pretend you are a waterfall and show me how you move.
7. Pretend you are a tree in a storm. Show how you would bend and sway in the wind.

Movement education can be a rewarding experience for children, especially when it is initiated in the first and second grades. Various media may be incorporated into movement education

40

and there are an infinite number of ways in which children can explore, create, and experience movement. Concepts of space, time, distance, body shapes, and body awareness can be developed.

Vocabulary:

movement	practice	throwing
strategy	dodge	bobbing
rhythmic breathing	consecutive	movement
explore	create	education
experience	concepts	space
time	distance	body shapes
body awareness	quick	fast
slow	even	uneven
fitness	crawl	hop
curl	bend	jump
leap	warm up	stretch
high	media	low
near	far	

LANGUAGE ARTS

READING

Activities: Questions/

1. Read stories about exploration on the river, nature and wildlife, stones, soil, mountains, and other related topics. Lead a discussion of the related readings. Ask comprehension type questions.
2. Read stories such as Huckleberry Finn to the class during free time before lunch, and before going home.
3. Bring in interesting information about something you explored at the falls. Share it with the class.
4. Learn about famous explorers such as Columbus, Lewis and Clark, Ponce de Leon, Magellan, Daniel Boone, Davy Crockett, Vasco de Gama, George Washington, De Soto, Andrew Jackson, John Glenn, and others.
5. Develop a reading center containing a large area rug, library books, tape recorded stories, record player, story records, comic strips, flash cards, salt box, wildlife specimens, grocery store materials, magazines, and task cards.
6. Make a list of class activities from the field trip. Pass out work sheets and have the children number the events in order of occurrence.
7. Learn how to use the dictionary. Look up the following words: exploration, alphabetize, sequence, Haiku, Diamante, Cinquain, diagonally.

Vocabulary:	language arts	related	topics
	discussion	comprehension	information
	Huckleberry Finn	famous	explorers
	Columbus	Lewis and Clark	Magellan
	Ponce de Leon	Davy Crockett	Daniel Boone
	Vasco de Gama	specimens	De Soto
	Andrew Jackson	John Glenn	develop
	George Washington	library	arrange
	include	events	order
	occur	sequence	dictionary
	alphabetize	Haiku	characters
	Cinquain	diagonally	dialogue
	scenes	acts	

WRITING

Activities:
Questions/

1. What would you be thinking if you were one of the trout swimming in the Cherry River? Write down some of your thoughts.

2. Write about a water machine you invented. Tell how it works, what it is used for, and why it is important to the world.

3. Begin an exploration story by asking them to write one or two sentences on a piece of paper. Pass your story on to other students so they can add something too. Be creative. Read the finished story to the class.

4. Find pictures of waterfalls from magazines or books. Write a descriptive paragraph about one picture. Share your paragraph with a friend.

5. Make a story book about the field trip.

6. Write a Haiku or Cinquain about nature. What is a syllable? What is a synonym? What is a Haiku? Cinquain?

7. Make a crossword puzzle using field trip vocabulary words.

8. What is a Diamante? Discuss antonyms. Write a Diamante about something related to our field trip. Example--Found and Lost.

9. Make a bulletin board displaying children's Diamantes, Haikus, and Cinquains.

10. Practice upper and lower case manuscript letters using a stick in the sand, or scrape letters on the rocks.

11. Describe the appearance of a rock, mudhole, waterfall or something you observed today.

Vocabulary:	thoughts	machine	products
	descriptive	paragraph	storybook
	syllable	Cinquain	Diamante

42

crossword	synonym	antonym
Haiku	puzzle	related
lower case	display	upper case
bulletin	manuscript	appearance

SPELLING

Activities/
Questions:

1. Learn to spell new words related to the field trip. Alphabetize these new words and make a dictionary.
2. Have a spelling bee using the field trip vocabulary words.
3. Make up riddles or rhymes with spelling words. Share them with the class. Let them guess the answers.
4. Play Find-A-Word. Hand out work sheets containing "exploration" spelling words hidden either horizontally, vertically or diagonally. Circle the words as you locate them.
5. Make a spelling list necklace. Print a spelling word on each cardboard disk. When you learn to spell a word, add that word disk to your string necklace.
6. How many words can you make from the letters in "exploration"?
7. Add prefixes and suffixes to the words you made from "exploration" to make more new words.
8. What are prefixes? What are suffixes? Give five examples of each.
9. Make a lettergram using words you have cut from magazines. Glue them on paper. Give your letter to a friend.
10. Make alphagrams with your spelling words. Use alphabet noodles to spell the words and glue them on file cards.
11. Play "Alphabet Soup". Who will make the most spelling words from his alphabet soup?
12. Make a short story using all of the "exploration" spelling words. Share your story with a friend.

Vocabulary:

dictionary	riddle	rhyme
horizontal	vertical	diagonal
locate	print	disk
prefix	suffix	example
lettergram	alphagrams	quiz
spelling	paragraph	share

LITERATURE

Activities/
Questions:

1. What are folk tales? Learn a folk tale about exploring in the woods. Share it with the class.
2. Who was Robin Hood? Where did he live? What did he do? Who was his companion on many adventures?
3. Who was Mike Fink? For what was he famous?
4. What are fables? What is the moral of a fable?
5. Who are the usual characters of fables? Tell several fables to the class. Can you tell some lessons they teach? What is your favorite fable?
6. Tell your version of a fairy tale or modern fanciful story.
7. Make up fables, probably similar to ones already told. Let other pupils guess the moral of the story.
8. Who was Johnny Appleseed? Where did he travel? For what was he famous?
9. What are fairy tales? What is the difference between fables and fairy tales?
10. Read _Alice in Wonderland_. What was Alice's adventure and what did she explore?
11. Who was Peter Pan? Where did his adventures take place?
12. What brothers are famous for writing fairy tales? Read several "Grimm's Fairy Tales" to the class. What is your favorite fairy tale? Why?
13. Read exploration and adventure stories such as: "Robinson Crusoe", "Peter Pan", "Alice in Wonderland", "Captain Kid", "Wizard of Oz", "The Merry Adventures of Robin Hood", "Rip Van Winkle", "Moby Dick", "Swiss Family Robinson", and "Bambi".
14. Share your favorite Walt Disney story with the class.
15. For what is the Caldecott Award given? What are illustrations? Do you think library books with the Caldecott award seal deserve it? Which ones? What is an allegory?

Most children's literature could be read in relation to the theme "Exploration at Cherry River Falls", since the characters are primarily animals and their adventures are usually out of doors.

Vocabulary:

| literature | folk tale | fairy tale |
| Robin Hood | Sherwood Forest | tall tale |

Mike Fink	lumberjack	Babe the Blue Ox
Paul Bunyon	boatman	fable
moral	Aesop	animals
modern fanciful	similar	Johnny Appleseed
Alice in	Peter Pan	Never Never Land
Wonderland	Robinson Crusoe	Wizard of Oz
Grimm	Captain Kid	Rip Van Winkle
Moby Dick	Bambi	Newberry
Swiss Family	Caldecott	distinguished
Robinson	illustrations	seal
award	Walt Disney	theme
author	allegory	

LISTENING

Activities/
Questions:

1. Close your eyes. See how many sounds you can hear in a two-minute period. Make a list of the things you heard.
2. Listen carefully to the symphony of sounds at the falls. Can you hear the water? Birds? Trees? Pick out one source and listen to it carefully.
3. Play several listening games such as "Simon Says", "Mother May I", "I Am Going to the Moon", "Fish Swim, Frogs Jump", "Number Game", "Verbal Tennis".
4. Listening to the sounds around you, distinguish one sound you hear. Describe it orally and have other children guess what makes your sound.
5. Listen to several different recordings of water-falls. Imagine what the waterfalls look like from their sounds.
6. Is the waterfall high? Small? How can you tell? What are the differences in the sounds? Is the water falling heavily or lightly?
7. Play different forest animal sounds. Identify the sounds.
8. Put your ear to the ground. Listen. What do you hear? Can you listen under water? Find out.
9. Can you listen to trees, flowers, or animals grow? What can you hear growing?
10. Would you rather listen than talk?
11. Put several objects collected on the field trip in a bag. Shake an object in the bag. Can you recognize the sound and identify the object?

Vocabulary:

period	listen	symphony
verbal	directions	distinguish

45

recognize   identify   oral
imagine   sounds   objects

DRAMA - SPEECH

Activities/
Questions:

1. In class, have children do their own thing with
   the following beginnings:
   --One day while I was playing at the falls. . .
   --As I was carefully crossing the fall wall, I
   saw the slimy moss. . .
   --I look into the water and. . .
   --I was going to sleep on a rock in the hot sun,
   when the rock said. . .
   --I was playing in the sand and a big fish. . .
   --I was digging deeper and deeper into a mud-
   hole and you wouldn't believe what I found. .
   --The neatest thing I explored today was a. . .
   --As I was examining a fishworm, it . . .
   --If you look closely at soil you will find. . .
   --I was sitting under the pine trees playing in
   the needles, and I heard one tree whispering
   to the other trees. . .
   --The forest's animals biggest complaint about
   people is. . .
   --If you want to show plants you love them you
   have to. . .

2. Fill a paper bag with several things collected
   on the field trip. Begin telling a story, pull
   an object from the bag and include it in your
   story. Pass the bag to another child so he can
   continue the story in the same manner.

3. Pantomime a creature or object you observed at
   the falls. What are you?

4. Present an elementary class play. What is
   dialogue? Act? Scenes? What are characters?

5. On file cards print _a_, _e_, _i_, _o_, _u_.
   Write your trouble consonant sound before and
   after each vowel. Repeat each syllable three
   times.

6. Make a work sheet with "exploration" words.
   Circle each word that: (1) begins with your
   trouble sound; (2) ends with your trouble sound.

7. Can you say your trouble sound at the beginning
   of words? End of words? In the middle of
   words?

8. In your spelling book, find ten words ending
   with your trouble sound, and ten words with
   your trouble sound in the middle of the word.

Vocabulary: drama   speech   beginning
             middle   ending   pantomime
             continue   creature   elementary
             play   dialogue   act
             scene   characters   vowels
             consonants

NON-VERBAL COMMUNICATION

Activities/   1. Take pictures of pupils exploring or observing.
Questions: Discuss expressions in class.
              2. What does verbal mean? What does the prefix
                  "non" mean? Do you know what non-verbal means?
              3. What is communication? How many ways of com-
                  municating non-verbally can you think of?
              4. How do Indians communicate non-verbally?
              5. Observe animals, especially fish. Do they com-
                  municate non-verbally? How can you tell?
              6. Do cars communicate non-verbally? To whom do
                  they communicate? How? What about boats?
              7. What can rocks communicate non-verbally? Land?
                  Clouds?
              8. Show film on non-verbal communication. Count
                  all the objects you see communicating non-
                  verbally.
              9. Does your teacher communicate non-verbally with
                  you? How? When?
             10. Do forests communicate non-verbally? What do
                  they tell you?
             11. What are facial expressions? Demonstrate.
                  What does each one say?
             12. What is body language? Discuss. Demonstrate.
                  What are you saying in each position? What is
                  eye behavior? Discuss these and demonstrate.

Vocabulary: non-verbal   communications   expressions
             smoke signals   facial   demonstrate
             body language   eye behavior   contact
             gestures   position

GRAMMAR - SLANG - DIALECTS

Activities/   1. Make up sentences about exploration. Divide
Questions: them into sentence phrases on flash cards.
                  Combine phrases together to make new complete
                  sentences.
              2. What are words like Daniel Boone, nature, water-
                  falls, fish, dirt, and flax called?

47

3. What are words like tall, green, leafy, muddy, dirty called?
4. What are words like growing, chirp, blows, dig, explore, climbing, find, and look called?
5. What is slang? Discuss a few slang terms in relation to nature.
6. What are dialects? Do you know someone who talks differently than you? How do they talk differently?

Vocabulary:

divide	sentence-phrases	complete
nouns	verbs	slang
dialects	adjectives	

TIN CANS

Becky Burris

SCIENCE

Activities/ Questions:

1. Put some dirt in the bottom of a can and plant a seed in the dirt. Place the can in the sunlight and water it each day. What appears?
2. Take two cans and put a hole in the bottom of each. Tie a long string through the cans. Find a buddy and each of you take one of the cans to opposite ends of the room. Can you hear each other talking through the cans? Does sound travel along the string? If so, how?
3. What kinds of birds did you see at the "can" bird feeder? Make a chart and record your findings. What color were the birds? Draw a picture of a bird and label its parts. What kind of food do the birds like best? At what time of the day do most of the birds appear? Can you tell the mother birds from the father birds? How?
4. Fill a large can with water. Drop a sponge, a twig, a piece of cardboard, a marble, a block, and a piece of cotton into the water. Which of the objects float? Why?
5. Take an empty paint can and put some water inside. Put a fire under it and put the top on it after the water boils. What happens? Pour cold water over the heated can. Can you explain what occurs?
6. Fill a can with water. Use a straw to draw the water out of the can. What makes the water come through the straw?
7. Put some liquid soap in a can of water and blow into the water with a straw. Watch the bubbles form. What causes the air bubbles?

8. Will a can float upright in water? Why or why not? Try this.
9. Place a can upright in a tub of water. How much water does it take to fill the can before it will sink? Why?
10. Submerge a can upside down in water. Will the can stay under the water or come to the surface? Explain why.
11. If you have a can that will hold one pound of sand, will it hold one pound of feathers? Why?
12. Take a can of pop, a can opener, and a pan. Put one hole in the top of the can. Turn it up to pour the pop into the pan. Now put another hole opposite the first. Now what happens when you pour out the contents? Which is faster? Why?
13. Fill a can with water. Place a piece of note-book paper on top. Invert the can, and the paper sticks. Why doesn't air flow out of the can?
14. After cans are discarded and exposed to weather, what happens to them?
15. Scrape one area on two cans with a knife. Expose one can to air and submerge the other can in water. Watch these cans for several days. Which will rust first? Why?

Vocabulary:

dirt	twig	seed
marble	sprout	block
water	cotton	moist
float	sun	sink
hole	tin	string
paint	telephone	fire
sound	boils	ear
vacuum	noise	air pressure
bird	straw	robin
soap	bluejay	bubbles
beak	full	feet
empty	head	oxidation
feathers	pound	food
rust	tail	sand
blue	volume	red
weight	sponge	flow

MATH

Activities/ Questions:

1. Count the number of beans in the can. Can you divide these into six equal groups? How many do you have in each group?
2. Weigh the can with the metric scale. How many grams does it weigh? Now fill your can with

49

water. Weigh the can again. How many grams does the water weigh?

3. Pick a can from the box. How tall is it in decimeters? In centimeters? In millimeters?

4. Choose the can from the group which is the largest. What do you suppose was inside this can? Which can is the smallest? How many small cans of sand does it take to fill the large can? What fractional part of the large can is the small can?

5. Can you make a balance using two cans? How can you use the balance?

6. Go to the play store and buy as many cans of food as possible with $2.50. Did you have any money left? If so, how much?

7. Sort the various cans into sets with common characteristics. How many cans do you have in each set?

8. Allowing each can to represent one unit, show how you can subtract 23 - 19 using regrouping.

9. Use cans to make a bowling game. Play with two or three friends and keep score. Each can that is knocked down is worth four points.

10. Put 12 dice into a can. Shake the can and pour out the dice. See how many addition and subtraction facts you can make from the numbers shown on the dice.

11. Label 26 cans with letters of the alphabet. Under each letter put the monetary value of the can, such as A - 1¢, B - 2¢, C - 3¢ . . . Z - 26¢. How much does your first name cost? How much does your last name cost? Which costs more? Find a word that costs $1.00.

Vocabulary:

add	cent	subtract
store	multiply	buy
unit	set	regroup
divide	change	number
meter	bowling	decimeter
score	centimeter	round
gram	circle	weigh
triangle	liquid	square
millimeter	cube	size
blocks	large	count
small	same	medium
dice	big	cost
little	difference	sand
sum	fraction	balance
money	dollar	

Activities/
Questions:

1. Look in the dictionary and find as many words as possible that contain "can". Write each word on a notecard and learn to spell it.

2. Read The Little Engine That Could. How is the word "can" used in this story? What do you think the little engine meant when he was using the word "can"?

3. Write a story about the can family which you made in art.

4. Put on a puppet show using can puppets and writing your own dialogue with members of your group.

5. Look at the assortment of cans on the table. Finish each sentence: A can is _____. A can smells like _____. A can feels like _____. A can tastes like _____ _____.

6. Pretend you are a can of beans on the grocery shelf. Write a story about your life.

7. Write a Haiku poem about a can.

8. Have two cans labeled "subject" and "verb". Provide cards in each. Pick a subject card and a verb card from the cans. Make a sentence using these words.

9. Label 26 cans with letters of the alphabet. Make as many words as possible from your can letters. Have a friend see how many words he can make from the cans.

10. Using your "telecans", write a conversation you might have with a buddy.

11. What do the labels on cans tell you? See how many different labels you can find. Where were the contents of these cans produced?

Vocabulary:

dictionary	sentence	engine
alphabet	whistle	conversation
hill	talk	valley
listen	train	speak
yard	polite	country
answer	mother	labels
father	produce	brother
sister	cousin	puppet
stage	curtain	shelf
high	grocer	sack
poem	Haiku	subject
verb		

Activities/
Questions:

1. From what are cans made? Are they made in different countries? Why were cans invented?
2. What is shipped to the United States in cans? From what country is this sent?
3. Explain how farmers use cans. If possible, visit a farm and write a story about what you observe.
4. What is your favorite food that comes in a can? Where is this food manufactured? How does it get to you?
5. Design a different can to represent each of the following countries: France, England, Switzerland, United States, and Japan. How are you able to tell which can belongs to which country?
6. Make a can train. When did the first train appear? Who were the men responsible for it? Where did it travel?
7. Make a replica of Jamestown out of cans. Explain the first settlement there. How might life have been different for these people if they had used the can?
8. How do industries use cans after they have been discarded?
9. What states have the raw materials for cans?
10. How do housewives use cans?
11. Are cans more beneficial to us than bottles? Why?
12. Which is better to use -- a tin can or an aluminum can? Why?
13. Make a film on the process of canning. What foods are canned at home? Are they safe to eat?

Vocabulary:

material	recycling	tin
industry	milk	cook
cows	aluminum	farmer
film	truck	canning
food	rail	France
England	Switzerland	United States
Japan	Eiffel Tower	mountains
chop sticks	statue	snow
clock	track	settlement
Indians	Pilgrims	feast

MUSIC

Activities/
Questions:

1. Label your cans with Do, Re, Mi, Fa, So, La, Ti, Do. Arrange them in the correct order. Can you sing these syllables?

2. Using the piece of music provided, arrange your syllable cans in the proper order to correspond with the scale.
3. With a small group of friends, choose cans which have musical note names on them. Arrange yourselves to form a simple melody. Can anyone play this tune on the piano?
4. Make a simple xylophone from cans and label each can with a note. Can you play a melody on your xylophone?
5. Fill some cans with beans and cover both ends tightly. What kind of an instrument have you made? Can you use your instrument to keep time with the melody on the record?
6. Make a tom-tom from a large can. Pretend you are Indians and make up a war dance using your tom-toms to keep time.
7. Take some old tin cans and make a musical chime to hang outside.
8. Work together on forming a can band. What instruments will you need that can be made from cans?

Vocabulary:

scale	staff	syllables
line	music	space
song	clef	tone
treble	rhythm	bass
harmony	quarter	melody
half	sing	whole
play	piano	voice
xylophone	instrument	shaker
record	Indian	dance
movement	chime	notes
rest	up	down

ART

Activities/ Questions:

1. From the materials available, make a "can family" and label each with a name containing the word "can".
2. Make "can puppets" to be used in a puppet show.
3. Take a large can and make a bird feeder out of it.
4. Using cans, make a large tin man.
5. Using water colors, draw a happy can and a sad can.
6. What can you make using a can? Invent a new toy.

7. Melt some candle wax and pour it into your can Put a wick in the wax. When the wax is hardened, remove it from the can.
8. Draw a cartoon with can characters.

Much of the physical matter that is appropriate for learning centers will be suitable for various stages of child development. The important thing is that the suggested activities for the centers be in keeping with the developmental levels of the children involved. Some of the factors to be considered before learning centers are ready for use by children are:

1. Is the physical matter safe for the developmental level of the students.
2. Can the students follow written suggestions?
3. Can the students keep a written record of their behavior in the centers?
4. Have you structured the environment so it is physically suitable for the children's developmental level?
5. How much orientation will be required?

Properly structuring the environment includes such things as whether a particular piece of matter will interest the child. A five year old may not be as interested in building castles or something with blocks. A ten year old will probably resent matter such as ABC blocks which are usually associated with nursery age children. After using your professional judgment, the trial and error method will be reliable because the matter in the centers is never fixed. Old stuff is constantly being removed and different stuff should be placed in the centers periodically. If the children reject it, throw it away.

The prereading child will have to be guided verbally and through the nature of the physical matter in the center. Students who are able to read and write can begin to follow written suggestions and they can make some effort at keeping their own behavioral records. Upper level students will probably be able to follow written suggestions and keep records of their own behavior. A wide array of suggested activities, things the students can do in the centers, should be available for those who are able to follow written suggestions. The activities could, for example, be recorded on small cards and filed in the center.

The question of orientation depends on the developmental level of the children. Children at the first level (K-3) need less orientation than more experienced children who are often accustomed to sitting still and being told what to do and what not to do. With younger children the orientation can be compared to a situation where a three year old is in an austere room. He will soon drive himself and anyone else around, crazy. Provide the child with a tricycle, a teddy bear, or a pull toy, however, and the situation will change immediately. Younger children will fall right into the structure of the center. Patience is important during the orientation period for middle and upper level students. They may keep bugging the teacher about what to do or needle each other in the centers. Give them plenty of time: encourage them to seek solutions to problems on their own; suggest they ask a friend in the center for help; and tell them constantly that they are doing fine, that you like them just as they are. From six to twelve weeks should be allowed for children in the middle and upper levels (grades 4-6) to become competent in center activities.

Most teachers who are attempting to convert a traditional classroom to learning centers will probably want to make the transition a gradual process. So the number of centers one has ready is a big factor in the administrative procedures involved in center implementation. A teacher who begins with one center should make it a vital part of the total program rather than an adjunct extra that is used in spare time, for rewards or for only those students who have completed regular assignments. Every child in the classroom should have an opportunity for equal time in the center. Also, no ability grouping should be imposed upon the center population.

If one center will accommodate six children, up to six children could be in the center at any given time throughout the school day. To begin with, a system might be used whereby students occupy the center on a rotating basis. At the beginning of the school day, six children could be selected by lot to play in the center for a maximum period of time. A given child should be allowed to leave the center at will and return to other activities. If one child leaves the center during the middle of the period, another child should be able to go from another classroom activity to the center. Fairness should be employed by the teacher so that each child feels that he is getting his share of time in the center.

The major administrative problem that one center poses for teachers is the belief that the students who are in the center will "miss" something vital being learned by the group of students not in the center. Consider that if the center happens to be a math center, the students should be able to learn all of the program concepts of this discipline in the center. This means that it should be possible to drop math from the regular daily program of subjects which are taught in large group situations.

When two centers are activated, e.g., math and language arts, approximately one half of the curriculum should be available through the center activities. As additional centers are added, time will be picked up from the traditional program. One should never try to make centers function while the existing program is kept intact.

The primary goal when implementing learning centers, should be to get the total program to function through at least five centers which accommodate the major disciplines, and to utilize the overflow area for miscellaneous activities. Individual privacy areas such as carrels should be provided. When using the total center approach, a good way to organize for self direction is to identify each center with a color coded pass. One could, for example, paint six tongue depressors red, six blue, six green, six yellow, six orange, six pink, and one or two black (used for private carrels). Of course other devices and colors may be used. These devices should be placed in a rack inside the room where children can see them from anywhere in the room and reach them easily. Under the total center system, as the children come to school in the morning each child selects a color coded device that permits him to enter the center that is identified by the color he has chosen. As the devices are depleted, the children learn that they must take a color that is open and wait until a device has been returned to the central rack before they can enter a given area. This method gives the children controlled freedom in selecting the center they wish to be in and the length of time they wish to spend there. The children should be given the opportunity to prove that they will make wise decisions and that they will sample the total curriculum according to their individual needs and wishes.

Normally, most students will do an adequate job of programming their time and activities. Only after everyone is given a chance to function, should the teacher intervene through guidance and encouragement to find out why a few individual children may be neglecting one or more of the centers and over utilizing others. These few children should be counseled individually and helped to see the benefits in a more comprehensive program. It is always the case that one child does not need as much time at some centers as others and this individualization process should be encouraged. When a child apparently needs more time in a center than he is willing to voluntarily give, a good way to approach the problem is to ask the child if there is something wrong with the center matter or activities as far as he is concerned. Ask the child whether there is anything which could be placed in the center that would make it more attractive to him. This approach accommodates the important human dimension and does not imply that there is anything wrong with the child.

WHAT CHILDREN DO IN CENTERS

An important objective in center learning is to facilitate the natural growth and development of each child and to accommodate the best knowledge available about how children learn. The classroom program then becomes twenty-five or thirty individual programs and the various objectives are attacked by each student in his own way within and among the centers.

With the assumption that action preceeds thought or learning, children are first permitted to explore the matter and the suggesed activities within the learning centers. Pre-planning consists essentially of getting the centers physically ready, or organizing for movement among the centers, and of providing suggested activities for the students in writing or on tape. The concept that the environment communicates significant messages to its inhabitants is an integral part of an effective center. If one places color cubes in a center, children will automatically begin to stack them as high as they can, build various geometric designs which each child will see as something different, or accomplish other educational tasks. They may identify colors, sort, classify, count, trade, and do all sorts of activities. If the center environment, with appropriate matter in the form of chairs, rugs, tables, and child-oriented decorations, can communicate to children that they are in a small world much like one they themselves would create, the children will probably respond positively to these messages.

The idea is that first kids go into the several centers and mess around with the items that are available and then move into the suggested activities that are prepared by the teacher. One does not assume, for example, that a child in the age eleven to thirteen category can build a 3x3x3 cube. The teacher may suggest in the activity file that children might want to try to do this. As the children respond to the suggested activity, the teacher will, through close observation and other means, detect those students who can perform a particular task. The teacher should make a written or mental note relative to the activity and each student's performance. After this process a significant plan can be developed by the teacher to encourage those students who have difficulty with a task to first seek help from other students and secondly from the teacher. By establishing a system such as the one described, individual progress can reach an adequate level within a classroom.

Learning centers are directed toward inquiry learning. Students become actively involved in a problem solving process instead of having ready answers available from the teacher or from textbooks. One way to consider the development of tasks for children in centers is for the teacher to take appropriate content and skill practices and convert them into modes that will fit center activities.

Learning activities should be designed to accommodate thinking ability in addition to the acquisition of a central knowledge base. As each child exercises his thinking process, through problem solving, learning games, and perceptual processes, individual sets of information and knowledge will automatically be sought by the learner. Thinking activities are encouraged through the use of open ended questions, problems that have several acceptable answers, creativity and fantasy, activities that help a child learn more about himself, matter that can be manipulated in various ways, and games such as checkers and chess. These kinds of thinking activities form the base of center programs and permit the acquisition of knowledge and skills to develop out of the given situations. A child, for example, who becomes interested in playing chess will probably want to learn more about the game. This desire should lead him to seek more information from other academic disciplines. His reading and math skills, moreover, may be increased incidentally.

The take off point for each discipline is from the center base. Rocks may be in the math center for children to sort, count, classify, and for building sets. When a child talks about a rock, however, he is finding out about language; when he draws or paints a rock, he is finding out about the arts; when he taps on several rocks with a stick, he is finding out about music; when he breaks a rock and looks at the pieces under a microscope, he is finding out about science; when he weighs rocks, he is combining math and physics; when he studies rocks, their formation, their disposition, rocks of our land and other lands, and how people use them, he is finding out about social studies; and when he relates to his peers and the teacher, he is at the core of the social and behavioral sciences.

The basic skills in reading and math can be attacked in centers just as other content and skills. Teachers should have no reservations about losing ground in these areas. If learning centers are working, children will learn to read, they will learn to add, and significantly, they will learn these skills as individuals in their own style and time. The constant procedure in your methodology and management is that the children will proceed from concrete matter to abstract thinking, or from induction to deduction. The child will see, feel, smell, and maybe even hear and taste words, phrases, and books before reading is demanded. He will take two rocks and place another rock with them before he is presented with the traditional pencil and paper addition facts. He may not need to memorize these facts directly but rather should learn them through involvement, need, and action. Children are going to get at most of the significant content and skills in learning centers. The only differences are that the classroom becomes informal, the environment becomes vitalized, the teacher becomes a learner and manager, the program becomes individualized, and the learning becomes more inquiry directed. Consider the following model:

1. A box of letters, words, and phrases is placed in a center.
2. Some children go into the center.
3. Each child takes from the box items of interest to him.
4. Each child plays with the matter in his own way (a group game may develop and should not be discouraged).
5. Some of the children may ask others questions about the matter.
6. The teacher observes each child.
7. The teacher asks questions and listens to the responses as he moves among the centers.
8. The children tire of an activity and change to other centers.
9. The teacher plans activities for the next day based on observation of the preceeding day. (Actually, one plans after the fact rather than before.)
10. The process begins again in other centers throughout the day; one day flows into another, and the children develop naturally without being diminished through failure, rejection, or ability grouping.

Learning centers are also ideal for a more functional utilization of audiovisual equipment. The major problem with devices such as television sets, film projectors, slide projectors, phonographs, tape players, and the like has been that they do not lend themselves to large group instruction with children. Since it is difficult to promote maximum learning through large group instruction, it follows that audiovisual equipment could be better utilized in a learning center. Rather than going through the hassle of showing A-V matter to some students in the class who are not interested at a particular time, teachers should consider keeping their A-V equipment set up so small groups could view the material at various times throughout the day. This method also contributes to another good learning practice: the students can learn to operate the equipment themselves.

A SELECTION OF PIAGETIAN TASKS

Beverly Ours

Among the many practical effects of the developmental research of Jean Piaget, the activity tasks are, perhaps, the most valuable to teachers. These tasks are characterized by being culture free and nonverbal. Therefore, they do not give an advantage in measuring the intellectual growth of children from varying backgrounds and cultures.

When utilizing these activities with children, teachers should not become anxious when a child cannot do the task as the teacher feels it should be done. The child's efforts should be accepted as sufficient because each child will reach a given stage (sensori-motor - birth; preoperational - age 6-7; or formal operational - age 11-13) at his own particular time. It is not a matter of right or wrong responses; it is a matter of practice and helping the teacher learn more about the kinds of lessons a child can perform and the kinds of experiences he needs.

The Piagetian tasks, in addition to being of value for educational measurement or diagnosis, are fun. Even if this is all teachers are able to gain from their utilization, the tasks are worth considering as educational materials. Kits to use for manipulation of the tasks are available commercially, but a resourceful teacher can build the equipment from scrap matter.

The following descriptions and illustrations of representative tasks which can be utilized with children were prepared by Beverly Ours as part of the requirements for a course the author was teaching.

1. Use a bottle partially filled with liquid. Ask the child to correctly draw the liquid, first when the bottle is tilted and then when it is turned upside down.

2. Practice in ordering: use line segments and ask the child to order them according to length.

3. Classification: Use geometric shapes of various sizes and colors. Suggest to the child that he classify these objects in as many ways as he can.
4. Provide pictures of horses and other animals. Ask the child to identify all the horses, then the animals. Ask which has more, the set of horses, or the set of animals.
5. Use red squares, blue squares, and blue circles, but no red circles. Use four boxes to classify the objects. Are all the circles blue? Are all the squares red?
6. Use a set of cards comprised of pictures of horses, trees, apples, and some blanks. Ask the child if the cards can be classified into two sets. This can help the child understand the null set.
7. Use three cups, two the same size, one larger. Say to the child, "If I were to give you some milk in a cup, would it be the same amount if I poured it into two cups?"

8. Use two balls of clay which weigh exactly the same. Change the shape of one ball of clay and ask the child whether one ball of clay weighs more. Conceptulization of this task shows that the child can conserve matter.
9. Use two sets of beads, each set containing the same number, and count the beads with the child. Change the order of the beads. Does the child understand that the number is still the same?

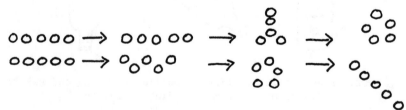

10. Show the child two sets of objects and ask him to dupli-
    cate the order of set one, using set two.
11. Reproduce sets in reverse order.

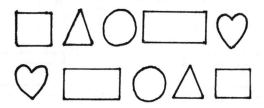

12. Show a set of wooden beads, ten brown and two white.
    Ask these questions: "Are there more brown beads or
    white beads?" "Are there more brown beads or wooden
    beads?"
13. Use four red flowers and two white flowers. Ask the
    questions: "Are there more red flowers or white
    flowers?" "Are there more red flowers or more flowers?"

14. Tell the child that one day he can have four pieces of
    candy in the morning and four more in the afternoon.
    The next day, because he isn't hungry in the morning, he
    can have one piece of candy in the morning and seven in
    the afternoon. Ask him which day will he get more can-
    dy.
15. Provide the child with a given number of objects. Ask
    him to divide them into two sets. Count each set. Put
    the two sets together and count them.

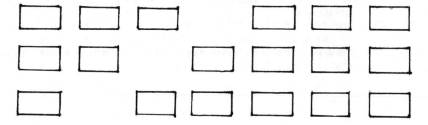

Once he has practiced this task, tell him that the objects are candy and ask him which would he rather have, the two sets or the combined set.

16. Use four identical sticks side by side with their end points aligned. Ask, "Are the sticks the same length?" Disalign the sticks and ask, "Are they still the same length?"

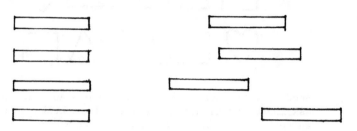

17. Use eight cups and eight eggs. Ask the child to place an egg in each cup. Remove the eggs and place them together in a set. Ask the child which has more, the set of cups or the set of eggs.

18. Put a model of three mountains on a table and seat a child and a doll on opposite sides of the table facing each other. Show the child a series of photographs of the model and ask him to choose the picture which would show the doll's view.

19. Provide two toy clothes lines and give the child some paper doll dresses, slacks, and skirts to hang on the line. Then ask the child to pick matching paper doll clothes from the table and hang them on the second line in the same order.

20. Arrange any group of objects in order according to certain characteristics, such as size.

21. Line up a row of buttons, chips, etcetera, and ask the child to make another row with the same number as yours (one-to-one correspondence).

22. String some geometric shapes and ask the child to repeat it. Have the child check his work by one-to-one correspondence.

23. Provide a table and two chairs. Place a box and a ball on the table. Ask the child to sit on the chair and draw what he sees from his chair. Then ask him to draw what you see from your chair.

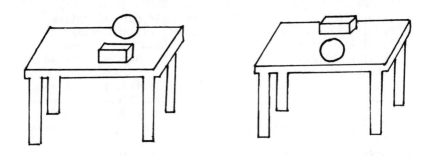

24. Seat the child across the room from a card table. Ask him to draw the table. Ask him to draw what he would see if he were on the ceiling.

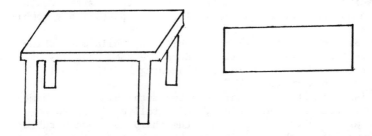

25. Ask the child to draw a view of a house, a car, a tree, and an ant as seen through a window in the floor of a plane when flying directly overhead.
26. Provide each child with a piece of paper which has an elephant and an ant drawn on the base line. Ask the child to draw a three leaf clover as it would look first to the elephant and then to the ant.
27. Combining objects to form classes: Place pictures on a table and assign the child a picture. Ask him to search for others that are like it in some way.
28. Multiplicative classification: Each child is given geometric shapes--small red squares and large squares, either red or green. Ask these questions: "Do all the small things belong in this box with the reds?" "Do the reds go in the box for squares?" "This is a box for small shapes; do the greens belong in it?"
29. In the center of a table, place pictures of red apples and strawberries, yellow bananas and grapefruit, orange oranges and pumpkins and pictures of miscellaneous non-living objects that are red, yellow and orange. Supply the child with three shadow boxes. Then: (1) Ask the child to collect pictures of fruit in one box and non-

fruit in another. (2) Have the child put all yellow fruits in one box, red ones in another, and orange fruits in another. (3) Have the child put all the yellow objects in one box, red in another, and orange in the third.

30. Have the child set up rows of 10 geometric figures varied in shape and color. Ask questions like: "Are all of the reds squares?" "Are all of the squares red?" "Are all of the triangles blue?" "Are all of the blues triangles?"

31. Have the child put green blocks in one ring, large blocks of varying colors in a second ring. The teacher slides one ring partly over the other. Ask the child what goes in the intersection.

32. Finding all possible combinations of two variables: Provide the child with two paper dolls and pictures of four yellow sweaters, four red sweaters, four blue skirts and four green skirts. He must dress the dolls in as many outfits as possible, not repeating any combinations.

33. Ordering Event: For this problem the child must think about how a pencil falls. "Here are some drawings of a pencil. Place them in order showing how the pencil would look if it fell."

34. Displacement of Volume: Use two metal blocks the same size but different weight, and a tall cylinder three-fourths full of water. Ask the child to place a rubber band around the cylinder at the place the water will be when the block is lowered into the water. Will there be a difference when the other block is put into the cylinder?

35. Conservation of Length: Use two straws. Start with both straws parallel. Change the position of one straw and ask the child if two ants were starting a hike at this end of the straw (point to the end) and walking at the same speed, would they both finish the hike at this point, at the same time? Would they both travel the same distance?

36. Conservation of Area: Present the child with two identical pieces of green construction paper. Tell him these represent fields or pastures. Place one toy animal on each piece of paper. Ask the child to compare the fields. Note that they are the same size. Comment that since they are the same size, each animal will have the same amount of grass to eat. Tell the child you are going to use blocks to represent barns. Place four barns on each field. With one group of barns together and the second group scattered on the field, ask the child which animal will have more grass to eat.

The tasks described above are designed to give teachers some indication about a student's development in the Piagetian sense. Most public school teachers deal with students who are in the preoperational, concrete operational, and/or formal operational stages. The kindergarten child is normally in the preoperational stage which, simply stated, means that his mental manipulation and conceptual development is limited in the number of events he cah put together about a given situation. The child cannot understand that the long, tall glass of liquid can be the same amount as the short, fat glass of liquid because he is overwhelmed mentally by the "fact" that the longer glass appears larger. He behaves on the basis of this intuition which is the logical way for a child at this stage of development to behave.

When a child reaches the age of six or seven he is usually able to do concrete operations. This means that his mind has developed to the point where he can cluster several events into a more functional deduction. He can understand that the person sitting on the other side of the table sees a different view because he can project himself into the other person's place.

Some children in the fifth and sixth grades and most adolescents function at the level of formal operations. This means that the child can do abstract thinking at a relatively high level. He can develop a clear understanding of such physical phenomena as how bicycle gears work and how time and the seasons pass. The adolescent at the formal operational stage is only different from an adult in his thinking abilities as far as experience is the thing that makes the difference relative to the ability to make intelligent conclusions. One should be cautioned here that even experience, however, does not guarantee a better conclusion.

Evaluation of learning center behavior relies essentially on observation and description by both the teacher and the students. One suggested evaluation model, since it places great emphasis on the children's observations, takes a form similar to the model below:

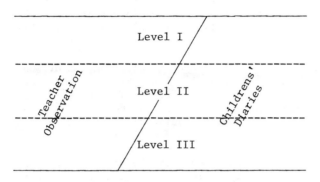

The basic evaluation form is one recording performance of a wide variety of cognitive and affective behaviors. The model indicates that since children in the first level will not be able to keep adequate diaries, the teacher must do more descriptive recording than is necessary in levels two and three. As the children move through the levels they will not be able to accept more responsibility for their own evaluation records and objectives. Since the movement is individualized and noncomparative, variations in who does what will also exist in each of the three levels.

Among the best ways to effect a meaningful series of evaluative criteria is to establish an open file folder for each child. The teacher and the child have access to this folder with no information being hidden from the child, no negative statements recorded, and no comparisons made with other children. If we assume that a child in level one is not able to record his behavior, then the teacher must take full responsibility for the records. The teacher must observe behavior carefully and daily note several behaviors for individuals. These behaviors should be written and placed in the child's folder. Additionally, the teacher must converse with each student periodically (two or three times each week) and add to the dossier the child's comments concerning what he has done. The folder should also be used to contain periodic samples of children's productions. Referring again to the evaluation model, as the children move through the levels and become more adept at keeping their own diaries, the teacher should play a less active role in determining the nature of the materials in the evaluation folder.

Some typical kinds of teacher recorded behaviors are such entries as: "Jimmy J. spent 30 minutes in the math center"; ". . . when asked to form two sets of three items, he built one set with three and the other with four"; ". . .used the word 'countdown' but spelled it differently than the center dictionary".

Children may make such entries as: "I helped Jerry with some glue he spilled"; "I didn't get done with the writing but hope to do it tomorrow"; "I learned how to follow a road map from my house to school"; "I spent too much time in the art center"; "Kevin pushed me in the lunch line. I don't think I like him. Nobody else likes him either."

These kinds of data together with samples of what the children are doing provide evaluation that fits center activities. The data are open, positive, progressive, nonthreatening (the child's entries are not corrected), and serve as a base for parent teacher conferences which should be an integral part of the evaluation process.

Other kinds of notebooks can be used for more categorized data. Each child may build his own dictionary of new words for spelling and meaning. A personal bound diary may be kept in addition to the file folder for general observations or for other specialized information.

Each child's behavior can be determined by the teacher through a periodic study of the recorded data and through individual conferences with the children. The children should be encouraged to be constantly moving toward more significant goals and they should be praised for their efforts. Mistakes which indicate effort should be viewed as an essential part of the learning process and should not be criticized in a negative manner. Mistakes can even be praised at times.

Standardized tests and letter grades should be dealt with pragmatically. It is probable that these kinds of traditional phenomena will have to be coped with even though it is hard to find evidence that they have made any significant contribution to helping kids learn. Comparative grading patterns such as ABC's are still very much an accepted part of most elementary school evaluation programs. If each child feels, however, that he is accepted by his teacher without reservation and that his teacher values learning beyond those items specified on grade reports, part of the pain that low grades cause can be soothed. A teacher in a system that demands comparative grading is asked to walk a tightrope between traditional grade reports and the needs of some children who cannot cope with convention. An honest communication from teacher to pupil that system policies, however questionable, must be dealt with, and that more humane ways of evaluation are being considered will appeal to most children.

Standardized tests including so called intelligence tests must be used in ways that will not prejudice the teacher toward a child or jeopardize a child's right to acceptance and confidence. Learning center programs demand that each child be seen as a person who already knows a great deal and who has the potential for becoming more productive. Even though things the child has learned in the past may not be congruent with middle class values, his current knowledge and behavior must be considered and accepted.

Another aspect of learning center management which leads directly to an evaluation procedure is the teacher-student negotiated contract. The most productive contract (sometimes called a plan) is between the teacher and one student so it is an individualized process. The teacher and the student enter into an initial agreement relative to the learning activities in which the student will be involved for a period of time. The time allowed for completion of the contract should depend upon the developmental level of the student and the nature of the learning involved. An example of a personal contract follows:

```
Student's name  _____
Subject  _____ Social Studies _____
Grade  _____
Date negotiated  _____
Date due  _____
```

A. Read chapter four from the basic text on how communities function.
B. In a selected reference book, read pages twelve through twenty which relate to the topic.
C. View the film, "Communities in Perspective", and the filmstrip, "Policemen at Work".
D. Write one half page about your readings.
E. List some questions you have after reviewing the suggested materials.

```
                              Student Signature  _____
                              Teacher Signature  _____
```

If the teacher and the student agree that three days would be an appropriate time frame for completion of the contract, this decision would be shown on the contract. During the working period of the contract, the student should be offered help and the teacher should be sure he has no logistical problems. The teacher should not, however, intervene in a negative manner through nagging or prodding until the end of the contract period. The student must take the responsibility for his own behavior and if the teacher observes that it is only an hour until the contract is due, and the student has not started his activities, the teacher should wait until the due time before the contract is discussed. When the contract is due, the teacher should examine the student's materials, have a conference with the student, and make future plans at this time. If the student has completed his plan, the teacher should reward him; if he has been irresponsible, the teacher should remind him that he has not fulfilled his signed agreement and if a sanction is needed, the necessary action should be taken. Whatever the result, a new contract must be proposed. If the student finished early, perhaps the next contract should be more challenging; if he did not finish, perhaps the contract performance agreement was overwhelming the student.

Other types of student-teacher contracting have similar characteristics to the personal contract discussed above. Contracting with small groups of students or contracting with the entire class are also feasible methods of learning management. The small group contract is the most practical of the three. Teachers may not be able to find time to negotiate personal contracts for a large number of students and the large group contract is inconsistent with the utilization of learning centers.

Another possibility, especially for the teacher who is doing informal teaching, is to utilize a combination of the three types of contracts. Personal contracts could be negotiated with selected students using certain variables or on a rotation basis; small group contracts could be negotiated for the learning center activities; and the large group contract could be utilized for such routine matters as lunch counts, money collections, class changes, and et cetera. The results of the students' contracts whatever system a teacher utilizes can become the basis for evaluation techniques which are productive to both the teacher and the students.

The evaluation of informal classrooms in general, as far as their success as a schooling option, has shown that students do as well as or better than traditional students in the academic areas and basic skills as measured by standardized and teacher made tests. It has also been theorized that students in informal classrooms do better in the affective areas of education, self-reliance, self-concept, getting along with others, and decision making than students in traditional classrooms. These areas cannot be measured with any great skill but there is fairly solid evidence that informal classrooms, when successfully executed, yield positive results. One must consider that there are weaknesses in the measurement of academic areas as well. The fact remains that reading, writing, and arithmetic, the basics of education almost as old as the trees on the school ground, will not be neglected in a good informal classroom.

Learning Center Evaluation Criteria (score from 1-10)

Name _____

1. Semi-private area.	
2. Accommodates small groups.	
3. Stresses a particular broad discipline, e.g. math, language arts.	
4. Arranged to facilitate informality.	
5. Creative expressions of the children are displayed	
6. Whole classroom environment reflects a minimum of large group instruction.	
7. Assignments are inquiry oriented, individualized, self-directed.	
8. Stocked heavily with junk materials.	
9. Storage containers are evident.	
10. Physical matter has some reflection of the local culture.	

The above list of learning center criteria was developed by the author and is used to help students evaluate their centers. It is also used as a guide for judging learning centers by the author.

INFORMAL EDUCATION IN ACTION

An elementary school classroom that has successfully made the transition from a traditional program to a total learning center program will have some of the following observable phenomena:

1. Each child begins his activity as soon as he arrives in the classroom. There is no distinct time when school begins--it begins for each child as he arrives.
2. The classroom becomes a nerve center of activity. Children, busy at their individual and group projects, converse and move about the room at will within the management guidelines.
3. Children are constantly making decisions about their own individual learning pursuits and they are accepting responsibility for their choices.
4. There is a quiet hum of activity that is not noise but rather the sounds of learning--children on their own with guidance.
5. The classroom has the distinct appearance of a child's world. Sterility and austerity are replaced by walls, ceilings, and loose matter that communicate to children a feeling of fun and acceptance.
6. The teacher is free to move about and manage the environment. The teacher can stop and talk to visitors because their entrance into the room will have little or no effect on what is happening. A visitor can, in fact, become involved immediately in the learning situation.
7. An atmosphere of peace, fun, laughter, and happiness is observable.
8. There are no discrete breaks in program activities. Each child is programming himself so the need for class schedules and other group procedures, except for routine matters such as lunch, is absent.
9. Rather than no structure, as skeptics might believe, a highly advanced form of structure is apparent. The structure that shows is that of individual children merging with matter and knowledge; twenty-five individuals converging, each with a thousand learning variables.
10. Production by children rather than a teacher shows everywhere. Writings, art forms, models, crafts, posters, directions, instructions, and other media right out of the central nervous system of the students communicates messages of vitality.

77

EPILOGUE

> We are all involved in the condemnation of
> words, an age of words. We are shut up in
> schools and college recitation rooms for ten
> to fifteen years and come out at least with
> a bellyfull of words and do not know a thing.
>
> Ralph Waldo Emerson
> Circa 1850

The first information the author received on open education,
British style, came from Joseph Featherstone's articles which
originally appeared in the New Republic in 1969. The British
Infant Schools, as described by Featherstone, seemed to have the
vitality and the security which are congruent with good educational practices. Even though psychological openness and problem
centered activities had long been a part of the stated beliefs
about the American schools, it was the author's experience that
most schools had failed to reach their potential and implement
practices which were in keeping with their philosophies. It was
not clear what it was, but it seemed that the British were onto
something.

The College of Education at Marshall University closed its
laboratory school because the officials there felt that the school
was an unrealistic situation for practicum experience and that,
moreover, active participation in the public schools of the local
region would be desirable. As the focus of practicum experience
was directed off campus, it was assumed that the philosophical
base for informal learning would provide the theoretical impetus
needed to develop a significant program.

The personnel involved utilized the theories of John Dewey,
the Plowden Report, and the writings of Jean Piaget, who is probably the most influential contemporary learning theorist. The
popular materials of the free school proponents, including A. S.
Neill and Salli Rasberry, a west coast radical, were considered as
they applied to the local project. To lend respectability to the
venture, Jerome Bruner's works were read. Special attention was
given to Bruner's writings since 1970 and his basic congruence
with Piaget. Arthur Combs' theories on perceptual psychology and
his belief that school should be fun for students were also basic
assumptions within the emerging rationale.

Basic Selections From Emerson, by E. C. Lindeman (Ed.), Mentor
Book from New American Library, New York, 1954. Reprinted with
their permission.

Our program began at the practical level emphasizing performance rather than theory. The ideas of the theorists were translated into suggestions which could be readily understood. The risk of misinterpretation was accepted for what it was worth. Arthur Combs was taken at his word when he said that any discipline could be reduced to twenty-five or thirty principles, all the rest was detail. Among the interpretations which emerged were (with an emphasis on interpretation):

Montessori education can be compared to the way many people store their hand tools. The outlines of a saw, hammer, and so on, appear on the garage wall. The tools are matched with the outline and storage is complete. The popular heavy jigsaw puzzles for preschool children are based on a similar idea. Piaget would not go for this with children, because while playing the game might be fun and wholesome, the educational aspects can be overplayed. He would give them the puzzle pieces and let them create their own manner of putting the thing together. He would assume that when the child had reached a given developmental stage, he could take the pieces of a horse and make a horse.

Bruner and Piaget basically agree concerning the developmental stages of children and adolescents; however, there are several related points of controversy. The only incongruence the author has found is Piaget's belief that the developmental stages cannot be greatly accelerated through contrived experiences as opposed to Bruner's idea that vital educational programs in the early years of children can speed up children's cognitive development. One must remember, however, that Piaget is talking about large concepts such as reversibility (being able to conceptualize that 4 + 3 is the same as 3 + 4), rather than minor concepts such as counting which children may verbalize prior to conceptualization.

The perceptual psychology of Carl Rogers and Arthur Combs, closely related to the philosophy of existentialism, essentially means that each person constructs his own reality. Perceptual psychologists argue that no matter how one perceives an event or a circumstance, the individual perception comprises the truth for the person involved; and, moreover, his

80

behavior will be guided by his perceptions.
They believe, further, that lectures, demon-
strations, or threats of retaliation and coercion, will not cause a person to change the
rationale which controls his behavior. If
these assumptions are reliable, and the author
believes they are, it naturally follows that
behavior change in people is an extremely com-
plicated process and that the process is under-
estimated when one assumes that others can be
told what they should believe and do. The only
way one can get at behavior change which is not
a game of getting along by going along is
through significant first hand experiences.
If a child is threatened, for example, by persons from other ethnic backgrounds, it takes
more than information to change his perceptions. Active involvement, although often
totally impractical, would seem to be the only
way to educate for perceptual change.

The physical effects of the classroom and
the personal interrelationships of nonverbal
behavior lend a vital element to open education
and learning centers. Two classic books by E.
T. Hall, The Silent Language and The Hidden
Dimension, coupled with Dr. Charles Galloway's
work in teacher education are excellent refer-
ences in this area. These authors have postu-
lated that the hidden messages of the personal
and physical elements hold secrets of moving
from the antiquity of tradition. The message
contained in the studies of these writers from
anthropology and education is that the many
nonverbal messages sent by walls, desks, and
teachers, and received by students overrides
the verbal barrage of talk and print that is
sent out by educational personnel at every
echelon.

Jean Piaget is among other things a
theoretician whose statements are not easily
translated into terms and ideas which have
meaning for curriculum development. His ideas
are, however, important to anyone who is interested in contemporary education for children and adolescents. Among the implications
for curriculum development in Piaget's theories, the author has found the following:
given a choice between learning experiences
which have many potential solutions or answers,

and experiences which have one answer, the
divergent activities are more productive in
helping students improve their thinking ability. Playthings for young children and games
for older children are compatible with Piaget's
theories when they give students the opportunity to express their own creative ideas and
engage their personal interests. A jigsaw
puzzle which has only one solution would not
be as valuable for learning purposes as a box
of miscellaneous sizes and shapes which could
be put together in a thousand ways, any of them
acceptable.

Children do not have wrong concepts about
their environment. Their concepts are different
because of limited experiences and lack of ability to think abstractly. The child of five
thinks the moon is following him because this
is the way it appears. The judgment is an
intuitive deduction and no amount of "teaching"
can change the concept until the child reaches
the age of six or seven. It is no more naive
for a child to have this concept than it is
for an adult to believe his car is moving at
a stoplight when in reality an adjacent car is
moving. Intuitive perceptions can also dis-
orient adults. Children's concepts are valid
for them at the time of conceptualization and
the productivity of moving students into abstractions too soon is questionable.

It is apparent that if Piaget and other theoreticians are
right, concepts cannot be transmitted and each child must, finally,
form his own concepts. Each child must take in the experiences
and information to which he is intrinsically drawn and let the
concepts fall where they may. A concept, then, may be defined as
a concentration of information into a cluster in the central nervous system which, after clustering, causes a person to feel,
think, or behave in a given manner.

One of the best methods for dealing with behavior problems is
adapted from William Glasser's reality therapy. It consists of a
few simple guidelines and it is a way of dealing with others which
often obtains positive results. The method is premised on the
condition that the teacher and the student are friends. At least
the teacher is a friend of the student whether or not his friend-
ship is returned. It is a practice which communicates to the student that the teacher likes him as he is and is not withholding
his affection until the student shapes up. It is shown in the

teacher's ability to demonstrate a genuine concern for the students welfare.

When a behavior problem develops, the teacher deals only with the present behavior of the student. There is no bringing up of past incidents or any implications that the problem is habitual. The teacher attempts to get the student to make a value judgment about his present actions. Is the student's behavior helping anyone? Is it doing anything positive for anybody?

The student and the teacher try to develop a plan for different behavior by the student. This is an attempt to contract for more productive efforts. It must be a plan the student can live with and through which he can be successful. The plan does not, therefore, involve too much immediate change on the part of the student. The student is not asked to quit fighting for the entire year. He is asked to agree not to fight for one day. The plan is put in writing and signed by the student. If he completes his agreement, some type of reward is in order.

If the student does not complete his agreement, some of the following ideas should be considered. Teachers should use sanctions in lieu of punishment. A sanction is a policy or procedure which is known by the student in advance of its implementation. Examples of sanctions are such things as removing a student from his group, sending him home, confining him to given areas in the classroom or building, and similar measures. No punishment is involved. The student is not subjected to physical pain or to a withdrawal of affection by the teacher.

Teachers need a variety of strategies to utilize in maintaining acceptable behavior in the classroom. The strategy briefly mentioned above is only one of many and is presented as an example for consideration. In addition to Glasser, another good source for practical ideas about student behavior problems is Fritz Redl's book, The Aggressive Child. Redl lists and discusses seventeen techniques for dealing with disruptive children: planned ignoring, signal interference, proximity and touch control, involvement in interest relationship, hypodermic affection, tension-decontamination through humor, hurdle help, interpretation as interference, regrouping, restructuring, direct appeal, limitation of space and tools, antiseptic bouncing, physical restraint, permission and authoritative verbat, promises and rewards, and punishments and threats. Discipline problems are one constant in dealing with students, but most of the teachers with whom the author worked on informal classrooms had better discipline than they did when they taught in a more traditional manner. The flexibility, mobility, individualization, and other structural facets of open classrooms are, when properly managed, conducive to better behavior.

Some of the following procedures and processes from the informal learning program in which the author was active proved to be effective for teachers and students. There is no system or order to them. There may be a rationale implied.

The physical appearance of the classroom should be changed before one gets too concerned with learning theories.

Questions which have no right or wrong answers should be a vital part of the curriculum. "Who should be the governor of West Virginia?" "Whose picture would you put on the five dollar bill if you had the authority?"

Resource persons can be selected from a variety of backgrounds. Instead of "culminating units" exclusively with professionals from denistry and medicine, invite local storytellers, electricians, plumbers, banjo pickers, cooks, and the like into the room to display their wares and talents.

Go at informal learning gradually, to one learning center at a time. It is a difficult, tedious process and the older the children are, the more difficult it is.

Let the children in on all. Everything that is brought in, built, or displayed must be a project belonging to a child or to the class. It is theirs. When this is done, children are less likely to be destructive.

Small items of detail should not become problems. Tolerance of minor disturbances, and putting such things as lunch counts, attendance reports, picture money, and alphabetical lists of students into the background or using them as learning aids may be helpful.

Essentially follow the state and county curriculum, but do it one child at a time. A teacher is not violating state standards by encouraging individual students to progress at their own pace.

Be as self-sufficient as possible. Learn to repair audio-visual aids and search the building for equipment not being used. Ask

the authorities for as little as possible
which requires psychological defense or money.

The development of personal, inexpensive
teaching materials is important. With the help
of the children, create a wide variety of
questions and suggestions on task cards for
use by the children. Bring in paper stuff,
puzzles, pictures, games, and other items
which can be laminated and boxed under various
task and curriculum headings.

Use as many fun activities as possible.
Try things such as digging a hole, collecting
cans, going fishing, and gathering walnuts.

Work hard at caring and accepting every
student. No matter how repulsive a student's
appearance or behavior, care and acceptance by
the teacher are vital elements in an open
classroom.

Give one or two students instruction on
operating all of your audio-visual equipment.
Have them teach the other students how to do
it. Every student should be checked out on
the machines available.

Invite parents and other community resi-
dents to visit the classroom. Invite them to
become a part of it. A parent should be able
to walk into any classroom at will, except
during selected activities. One of the major
problems with American education is that professionals have often removed themselves from
the people. Professionals often argue that
the parents they need to see will not come in.
One reason they do not come is because they do
not feel a part of the system. They have been
rejected because they are not a part of the
community leadership. Teachers could take the
first step through home calls and by making
parents welcome in the classroom.

Motivation is not some mystical, charis-
matic phenomenon which can be possessed by a
teacher. There is no motivation outside the
self. The teacher can, however, bring in a
dead mouse and let some children meatball it
for science. This is motivation. Anyone can
do it or learn to do it. The myth that stu-

dents could be motivated by charisma should
be discredited.

Extended space utilization is important.
Classroom closets, coat rooms, and other nondescript areas often left for junk and storage
should be developed for student accommodation.
Outside the room, moreover, hallways and other
areas near the classroom can often be converted
into activity spaces. The outdoor areas adjacent to the school building should be utilized. Regardless of weather, outdoor learning
activities should continue throughout the
school year whether the area is a blacktopped
playground or a grove of cedar trees, because
the potential for student activities is im-
pressive.

Be alert to find new stuff and practical
ideas. Read a variety of educational and
general materials. Listen to other teachers
and people outside the profession for suggested activities. Go about the community on
evenings and weekends gathering junk for the
classroom. Ask the students and their parents
to send stuff to the classroom. Go to rummage
sales. Do not develop a list of concepts and
try to find things to help teach them. Find
things and see what concepts develop as the
students interact with the matter.

Learning centers worked, for some teachers, in some schools.
In those classrooms where a degree of informal learning remained
after the direct local support was gone, long term changes in
teacher behavior was effected. It is impossible to determine why
informal learning can go in one teacher's classroom while it suc-
cumbs to tradition in other classrooms. It is just as hard to
find these answers as it is to find out what informal learning
really is. One can only speculate.

It is the author's belief that the teachers who accept informal learning are those teachers who had a compatible personality type before they ever heard of the methodology involved. So
the only thing we really did was to unleash some skills and strategies which the teachers already possessed. All we told them were
things they already knew or had, at least, suspected for a long
time.

Teachers who survive in informal classrooms above the kindergarten level must also have the personal resiliance to transcend
the logical forces which counter informal education ideas. In-

stead of depending on public money to provide the wide array of matter necessary, they must scrounge matter in their own way. Instead of demanding that the principal grant unqualified support, they must gradually build their own base through obvious success and competence. Instead of being defeated by small, bureaucratic rules, they must beat the system at its own game by remaining strong and detached, autonomous professionals.

Informal education is no different from any other form of education in one respect: it has to fight for survival. The people who are skeptical about informal education have two arguments. One, it works for some children and it does not work for others. Two, it is unrealistic to think that the schools are going to be significantly different from the surrounding social systems which are often closed and insecure.

These two arguments are persuasive because they have a modicum of truth in them which is about as much as can be said for any argument. Consider the idea that informal learning works for some students. It is true that a selected number of students in a given educational setting will already possess some of the personal characteristics which informal education is attempting to encourage. They have positive self concepts. They can accept responsibility. They are cooperative and productive. In effect, they have already learned about informal education at home, in the streets, and perhaps, in kindergarten. Other students, however, do lack these characteristics. They are destructive. They cannot accept responsibility. It is difficult to establish situations which appeal to their interest, to give them a chance at self-motivation.

There are at least two philosophical approaches to the problems of informal education working well with selected students. School systems could provide informal classrooms for those students who are readily able to accommodate themselves to the program; other students could be placed in more traditional programs. The second approach to the problem would be to assume that every student has the potential to be productive in an informal classroom. With this approach, the tedious process of helping students learn to be self-directed through practice in informal classrooms must be considered. The persons involved, including parents, must be able to provide the methods and materials which are necessary.

The second argument against open education, that it is incongruent with society, must also be considered. Again, one must begin with a philosophical base. Should the public schools try to prepare students to adjust and survive in a society as it already exists? Should the public schools try to prepare students who will have a desire to change society, to mold it to fit their own goals and values to accommodate the existing order? Are there other options? These are questions and, again, they are age old arguments which have not been settled.

The public school teacher is close to a variety of people in the community. Yet the position of teacher is the weakest one in the educational network. It has the least pay, the least power, and the least prestige. If teachers believe in democracy, they are in positions, nevertheless, to make it work. They are the ones who can get to know the parents of their students, who can visit students in their homes, who can invite parents into their classroom anytime of the day.

Informal education can be supported and encouraged by the educational bureaucracies, the state departments, the local systems, and the federal government. It can be stimulated through teacher education programs which emphasize experiences leading to competence in informal learning. Its good and bad qualities can be reported to parents and the public in various ways. The future of informal learning, however, depends on the teachers. These are the professionals who finally get the job done. They are the people who implement programs and ideas rather than merely advocating them in theoretical treatises or administrative edicts. Wherever informal education exists, the persons whom we should congratulate or blame, depending on one's point of view, are the teachers themselves.

BIBLIOGRAPHY

Alder, M. E. and J. S. Bruner, "Some Educational Implications of the Theories of Jean Piaget", *Canadian Education and Research Digest*, December, 1964, p. 291.

Agee, James and Walker Evans, *Let Us Now Praise Famous Men*. New York: Ballantin Books, 1960.

Allen, R. U. "Grouping Through Learning Centers", *Childhood Education*, December, 1968, p. 200.

Allender, J. S. "Teaching of Inquiry Skills Using a Learning Center", *Audio Visual Communication Review*, Winter, 1969, p. 399.

Ashton-Warner, Sylvia, *Teacher*. New York: Bantam Books, 1963.

Ausubel, D. P. "Neobehaviorism and Piaget's Views on Thought and Symbolic Function", *Child Development*, December, 1965, p. 1039.

Bayles, E. E. *Pragmatism in Education*. New York: Harper and Row, 1966.

Berlyne, D. E. "Recent Developments in Piaget's Work", *British Journal of Educational Psychology*, January, 1956, p. 219.

Blackie, John, *Inside the British Primary School*. London: Her Majesty's Stationery Office, 1967.

Blaschke, Charles, et al. "The Performance Contract", *Educational Technology*, September, 1970.

_____, "What's Left When School's Forgotten? Process Approach to Education", *Saturday Review*, April 18, 1970, p. 69.

_____, "What Turns Kids On", *Saturday Review*, April 15, 1967, p. 67.

Branson, M. S. "Using Inquiry Methods in the Teaching of American History", *Social Education*, November, 1971, p. 776.

Brick, E. M. "Learning Centers: the Key to Personalized Instruction", *Audiovisual Instruction*, October, 1967, p. 786.

Brown, R. M. "Learning Centers", *Audiovisual Communication Review*, Fall, 1968, p. 294.

Bruner, Jerome S. "Skill of Relevance or Relevance of Skill", *Saturday Review*, April 18, 1970, p. 66.

_____, "The Process of Education Revisited", Phi Delta Kappan, September, 1971, p. 18.

_____, "The Will to Learn", Commentary, February, 1966, p. 41.

Buell, R. R. "Piagetian Theory Into Inquiry Action", Science Education, February, 1967, p. 21.

Carswell, Evelyn M. and Darrell L. Roubinek, Open Sesame. Pacific Palisades, California: Goodyear Publishing Company, Inc., 1974.

Cass, James, "A School Designed for Kids", Saturday Review, March 21, 1970, p. 60.

Casteel, J. Doyle and R. I. Stahl, Value Clarification in the Classroom. Pacific Palisades, California: Goodyear Publishing Company, Inc., 1975.

Channon, Gloria, Homework. New York: Outerbridge and Dienstfrey, 1969.

Chase, Larry, The Other Side of the Report Card. Pacific Palisades, California: Goodyear Publishing Company, Inc., 1975.

"Classroom Verbal Interaction and Pupil Learning", Reading Teacher, January, 1970, p. 369.

Cohodes, A. "Put it in the Middle and Call it a Learning Center", Nations Schools, March, 1966, p. 79.

Coles, Robert. "Growing Up Free", Appalachian Review, Fall, 1967, p. 11.

_____, "Some Children the Schools Have Never Served", Saturday Review, June 18, 1966, p. 58.

Collins, D. Wane and M. J. Collins, Survival Kit for Teachers and Parents. Pacific Palisades, California: Goodyear Publishing Company, Inc., 1975.

Combs, Arthur W. The Professional Education of Teachers. Boston: Allyn Bacon, 1975.

Congreve, W. V. "Learning Center: Catalyst for Change?" Educational Leadership, November, 1969, p. 140.

Dennison, George, The Lives of Children. New York: Random House, 1969.

Dewey, John, Experience and Education. New York: Macmillan Company, 1938.

Duckworth, Eleanor, "The Having of Wonderful Ideas", Harvard Education Review, March, 1973, p. 217.

_____, "Piaget Rediscovered", Arithmetic Teacher, November, 1964, p. 496.

Durant, Will, The Pleasures of Philosophy. New York: Simon and Schuster, 1953.

Elkind, David, "Giants in the Nursery: Jean Piaget", Educational Digest, October, 1968, p. 19.

_____, "Measuring Young Minds", Horizon, Winter, 1971, p. 32.

_____, "Piaget's Conservation Problems", Child Development, March, 1967, p. 15.

_____, "Piaget and Montessori", Harvard Educational Review, Fall, 1967, p. 535.

_____, and J. H. Favell, Studies in Cognitive Development: Essays in Honor of Piaget. Fairlawn, New Jersey: Oxford University Press, 1969.

Estvan, F. J. "Teaching the Very Young: Procedures for Developing Inquiry Skills", Phi Delta Kappan, March, 1969, p. 389.

Featherstone, Joseph, The Primary School Revolution in Britain. New York: Pitman Publishing Company, 1970.

_____, "Teaching Writing", The New Public, July 11, 1970, p. 11.

Frisk, Lori and N. C. Lindgreen, Learning Centers. Glen Ridge, New Jersey: Exceptional Press, 1974.

Foster, John, Discovery Learning in the Primary School. London: Limited Publishing Company, 1972.

Fulks, D. G. Learning Centers in Elementary Schools. Dubuque, Iowa: Kendall/Hunt Publishing Company, 1973.

_____, "James Agee on Education", Educational Forum, March, 1976, p. 337.

Furth, Hans G. Piaget for Teachers. Englewood Cliffs, New Jersey: Prentice Hall, 1970.

Galloway, Charles, "Teacher Nonverbal Communication", <u>Educational Leadership</u>, October, 1966, p. 55.

Gattegno, Caleb, <u>What We Owe Children</u>. New York: Outerbridge and Dienstfrey, 1970.

Gies, F. J. and B. C. Leonard, "Inquiry and Self-Directed Learning", <u>School and Community</u>, December, 1970, p. 8.

Ginnott, H. <u>Between Parent and Child</u>. New York: Macmillan Company, 1965.

Glasser, William, <u>Schools Without Failure</u>. New York: Harper and Row, 1969.

Goldberg, Steven, "Bob Dylan and the Poetry of Salvation", <u>Saturday Review</u>, May 30, 1970, p. 43.

Gorman, Richard M. <u>Discovery Piaget</u>. Columbus, Ohio: Charles E. Merrill, 1972.

Greer, Mary and Bonnie Rubinstein, <u>Will the Real Teacher Please Stand Up</u>? Pacific Palisades, California: Goodyear Publishing Company, Inc., 1972.

Gross, Beatrice and Ronald, "British Infant School: A Little Bit of Chaos", <u>Saturday Review</u>, May 16, 1970, p. 71.

_____, <u>Radical School Reform</u>. New York: Simon and Schuster, 1969.

Hall, Elizabeth, "A Conversation with Jean Piaget", <u>Psychology Today</u>, May, 1970, p. 25.

Hall, E. T. <u>The Hidden Dimension</u>. New York: Doubleday, Inc., 1969.

_____, <u>The Silent Language</u>. Greenwich, Connecticut: Fawcett Publications, 1959.

Herndon, J. <u>How to Survive in Your Native Land</u>. New York: Simon and Schuster, 1971.

Hertzberg, Alvin and Edward F. Stone, <u>Schools Are for Children</u>. New York: Schocken Books, 1971.

Holt, John, <u>How Children Fail</u>. New York: Pitman Publishing Company, 1964.

_____, <u>How Children Learn</u>. New York: Pitman Publishing Company, 1967.

Horton, L. and P. Horton, "Learning Centers: A Working Bibliography", *Audiovisual Instruction*, December, 1970, p. 60.

Inhelder, Barbara and Jean Piaget, *The Growth of Logical Thinking*. New York: Basic Books, Inc., 1958.

Jennings, Frank G. "Jean Piaget: Notes on Learning", *Saturday Review*, May 20, 1967, p. 81.

Kaplan, Sandra N. et al. *A Young Child Experiences*. Pacific Palisades, California: Goodyear Publishing Company, Inc., 1975.

Kohl, Herbert, *The Open Classroom*. New York: Random House, Inc., 1969.

Kuslan, Lewis A. and A. Harris Stone, *Teaching Children Science: Inquiry Approach*. Belmont, California: Wadsworth Publishing Company, 1968.

Lee, M. and R. Van Allen, *Learning to Read Through Experience*. Des Moines, Iowa: Meredith Publishing Company, 1966.

Lewis, James Jr. *Administering the Individualized Instruction Program*. West Nyack, New York: Parker Publishing Company, 1971.

Martin, John H. and Charles H. Harrison, *Free to Learn*. New York: Prentice Hall, 1972.

Massialas, Bryon G. and Jack Zevin, *Creative Encounters in the Classroom*. New York: John Wiley and Sons, 1967.

McCracken, Samuel, "Quackery in the Classroom", *Commentary*, June, 1970, p. 45.

Olenzak, K. R. "Learning Centers: The Teaching Approach That Makes Old Schools Like New", *Teacher*, February, 1973, p. 54.

Piaget, Jean, *The Child's Conception of Number*. New York: W. W. Norton Company, Inc., 1965.

_____, *The Moral Judgment of the Child*. Glencoe, Illinois: Free Press, 1948.

_____, *The Origins of Intelligence in Children*. New York: W. W. Norton Company, Inc., 1962.

_____, *Plays, Dreams and Imitation in Childhood*. New York: W. W. Norton Company, Inc., 1962.

Postman, Neil and Charles Weingaeten, *Teaching as a Subversive Activity*. New York: Delacorte Press, 1969.

"Pupil-Pupil Teaching and Learning Team", Education, February-March, 1971, p. 247.

Rapport, Virginia (ed.), Learning Centers: Children on Their Own. Washington, D. C.: The Association for Childhood Education, 1970.

Rasberry, Sally, The Rasberry Exercise. Freestone, California: Freestone Publishing Company, 1970.

Redl, Fritz, When We Deal with Children. New York: Free Press, 1966.

Redl, Fritz and David Winerman, Controls from Within. New York: Free Press, 1952.

Repo, Satu, This Book is About Schools. New York: Pantheon Books, Random House, 1970.

Rogers, Carl R. Freedom to Learn. Columbus, Ohio: Charles E. Merrill, 1969.

Rogers, V. R. "English and American Primary Schools", Phi Delta Kappan, October, 1969, p. 71.

_____, Teaching in the British Primary School. New York: Macmillan Company, 1970.

Rowland, F. "Americanization of Jean Piaget", Educational Forum, May, 1968, p. 481.

Ruesch, J. and Kees Weldon, Nonverbal Communication. Berkley, California: University of California Press, 1956.

Rugg, Harold O. and Ann Schumaker, Child Centered School. Chicago, Illinois: World Book Company, 1928.

Samples, Robert E. "The Impediment of Creativity", Saturday Review, July 15, 1967, p. 56.

Sava, Samuel G. "When Learning Comes Easy", Saturday Review, November 16, 1968.

Schmidt, V. E. and V. N. Rockcastle, Teaching Science with Everyday Things. New York: McGraw-Hill, 1968.

Schmitz, C. D. and E. A. Schmitz, "Individualized Contracting in the Elementary Classroom", School Community, May, 1972, p. 14.

Schmoderer, M. "Happy-Time Learning Center", Momentum, May, 1972, p. 38.

Schrag, Peter, "Education's Romantic Critics", Saturday Review, February 18, 1967, p. 73.

_____, "The Schools of Appalachia", Saturday Review, May 15, 1965, p. 70.

Schwartz, Ronald, "Performance Contracts Catch On", National Schools, August, 1970.

Shaplin, Jackson T. and Henry F. Olde, Jr., (Eds.), Team Teaching. New York: Harper and Row, 1964.

Sharp, Evelyn, Thinking is Child's Play. New York: E. P. Dutton Company, 1969.

Shaw, Peter, "Steinbeck: The Shape of a Career", Saturday Review, February, 1969, p. 10.

Silberman, C. E. Crisis in the Classroom. New York: Random House, 1970.

_____, "How the Public Schools Kill Dreams and Mutilate Minds", Atlantic, June, 1970, p. 83.

_____, "Murder in the Classroom", Atlantic, July, 1970, p. 82.

Singer, S. L. "Creative Use of Learning Space", Audiovisual Instruction, September, 1964, p. 423.

Skinner, B. F. "Why Teachers Fail", Saturday Review, October 16, 1965, p. 80.

Sloan, C. C. "Freedom to Make Mistakes", Childhood Education, November, 1967, p. 168.

Slobodian, J. and E. Stuart, "Reading Materials Center", Michigan Education Journal, May, 1966, p. 31.

Smith, Fr. and J. A. Mackey, "Creating an Appropriate Social Setting for Inquiry", Phi Delta Kappan, April, 1960, p. 462.

Stehney, Virginia A. "Why Multiage Grouping in the Elementary School", National Elementary Principal, January, 1970, p. 20.

Stenner, Jack and Michael H. Kean, "Four Approaches to Educational Performance Contracting", Educational Leadership, April, 1971, p. 721.

Stretch, B. B. "The Rise of the Free School", Saturday Review, June 20, 1970, p. 76.

Sylwester, R. et al. "Four Steps to a Learning Center", Instruc-
tor, June, 1967, p. 73.

_____, "The Teaching of Inquiry Skills Using Learning
Centers", Audiovisual Communications Review, Winter, 1969,
p. 399.

Thomas, Robert Murray and Sherwin G. Swartout, Integrated Teaching
Materials; How to Choose, Create, and Use Them. New York:
David McKay Company, 1963.

Tolstory, Leo, On Education. Chicago, Illinois: University of
Chicago Press, 1967.

Trump, J. L. "Independent Study Centers; Their Relation to the
Central Library", National Association Secondary School Principal Bulletin, January, 1966, p. 45.

Voight, Ralph C. Invitation to Learning; the Learning Center
Handbook. Washington, D. C.: Acropolis Books, 1971.

Voyat, Gilbert, "I. Q.: God Given or Man Made", Saturday Review,
May 17, 1969, p. 73.

Wakin, Edward, "The Return of Montessori", Saturday Review,
November 21, 1964, p. 61.

Way, A. "Reading Center Files Needs", Wisconsin Journal of
Education, April, 1967, p. 14.

Wiggintin, Eliot, The Foxfire Book. Garden City, New Jersey:
Archer Books, Doubleday, 1972.

_____, Foxfire Two. Garden City, New Jersey: Archer
Press, Doubleday, 1972.

Wolensky, G. F. "Application of Some of Jean Piaget's Observations to the Instruction of Children", Teaching Exceptional
Children, Summer, 1970, p. 189.

Woodruff, Ashel, Basic Concepts of Teaching. San Francisco,
California: Chandler Publishing Company, 1961.

Wright, J. C. "Helping Students Write Contracts", Journal of
Reading, April, 1972, p. 521.